THE BEST IN RETAIL CORPORATE IDENTITY

THE BEST IN

RETAIL CORPORATE IDENTITY

STAFFORD CLIFF

B.T. Batsford Ltd • London

A QUARTO BOOK

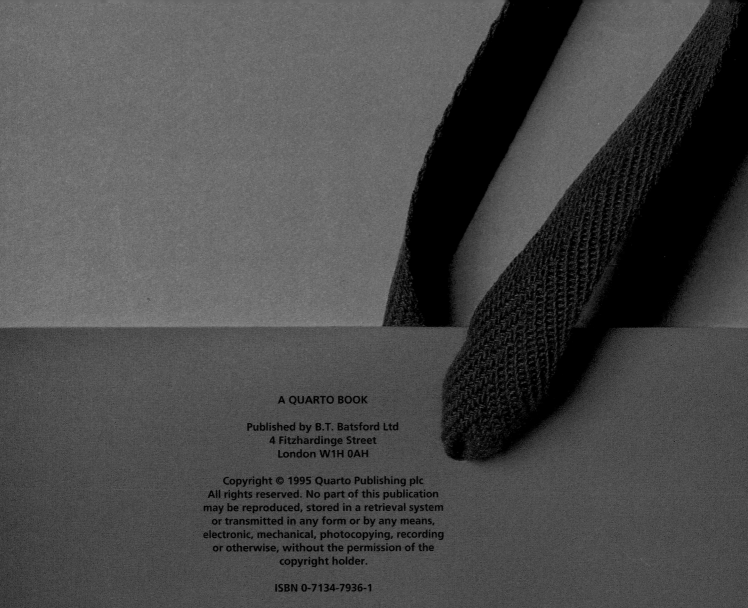

Published by B.T. Batsford Ltd
4 Fitzhardinge Street
London W1H 0AH

ISBN 0-7134-7936-1

This book was designed and produced by
Quarto Publishing plc
6 Blundell Street
London N7 9BH

Consultant Editor: Stafford Cliff
Project Manager: Katie Bland
Designer: James Lawrence

Typeset in Great Britain by
Central Southern Typesetters, Eastbourne
Manufactured in Hong Kong by Regent
Publishing Services Ltd
Printed in China by
Leefung-Asco Printers Ltd

*Stafford Cliff would like to acknowledge
the help of the following people
in the compilation of this book :
Jonathan Scott, Katie Bland, Sophie Hutchinson,
Valerie Lloyd, Kulbir Thandi, and Stephen Paul.*

Contents

Introduction by Stafford Cliff

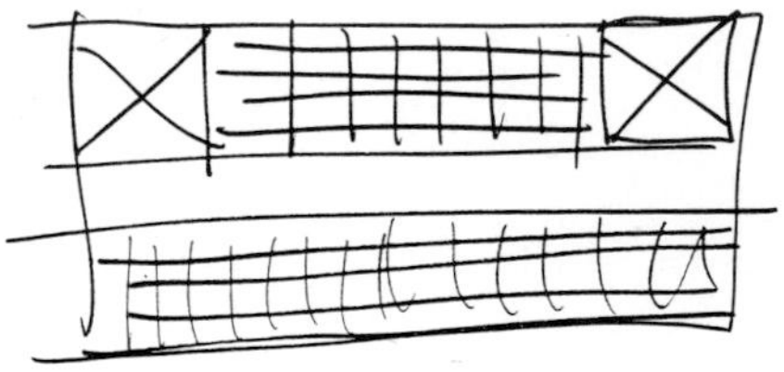

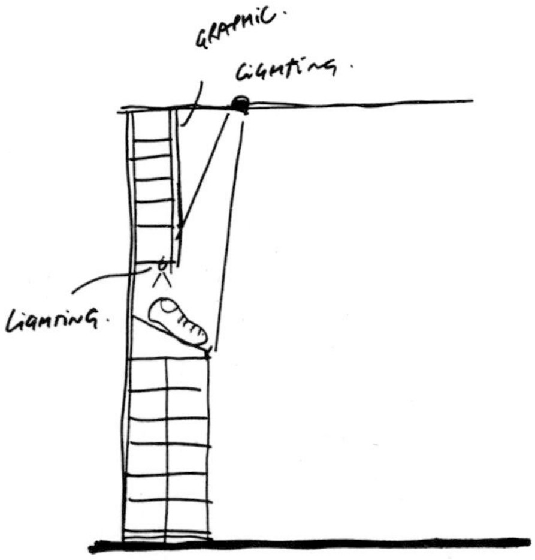

Dozens of quick sketches reveal how the system of shelving and individual display units began to take shape. Although the designers worked extensively on computer, the initial stage of the project was done more effectively with a pen and layout pad.

In the preparation of this book, I have visited hundreds of stores and collected material from some of the best design companies in Europe and around the world.

There is some spectacular work being done, and some innovative solutions. But inevitably, the picture of exteriors, interiors and shopping bags, cannot tell the whole story. How a shop works is just as important as how it looks, and how the solution was arrived at can be interesting too.

Design for retailing has changed a lot since the days when 'madame' could sit at a counter whilst an obliging assistant brought out the latest merchandise for her to consider.

Some might wish that those days would return. In the meantime, it's interesting to consider just how far we've come in the last 20 years. The 1970's and 1980's were a boom time for retailing. America was developing larger and larger out-of-town shopping malls, and converting dockland warehouses into themed shopping and eating environments, whilst the UK was busy rejuvenating its high streets and redesigning its chain stores.

Design companies spawned retail divisions with retail analysts, and lifestyle marketing was born.

In fact, Britain has always been known as a 'Nation of shopkeepers', so it's not surprising that although the 1980s recession hit many stores, it was often the ones who'd neglected to change with the times, such as old fashioned, oversized department stores, that suffered most.

Now shops are again opening with amazing frequency. Retail chains continue to test new concepts before 'Rolling them out', and management often expect new designs to last only as long as 2 or 3 years. Some retail chains even use a different design company on each of its branches, until they come to one they like or more importantly, one that 'works'. So while the days of the huge multi-discipline design groups are over, there's still plenty of work, internationally, for the retail specialist.

Some of these designers start life working in-house, for large retail organisations, before deciding to strike out on their own. Val Lloyd, and her colleagues Emma Starkin and Julie Manz are one such team. Val worked at Harrods, the famous Knightsbridge department store, as operations director of the Artistic division. She was responsible for co-ordinating the work of over 100 people in 4 groups within the store visual merchandising (display), graphic design, packaging, interior design and contract furnishing – and a division mysteriously called 'Artistic Design'.

Although Val is not a designer and never studied design – she was uniquely placed to learn the process, her practical approach to business quickly told her what would and would not work. Emma and Jo were also at Harrods when Val decided it was time to start on her own. In

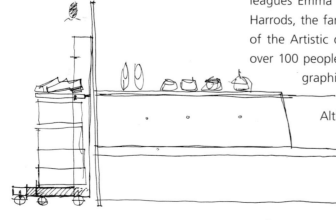

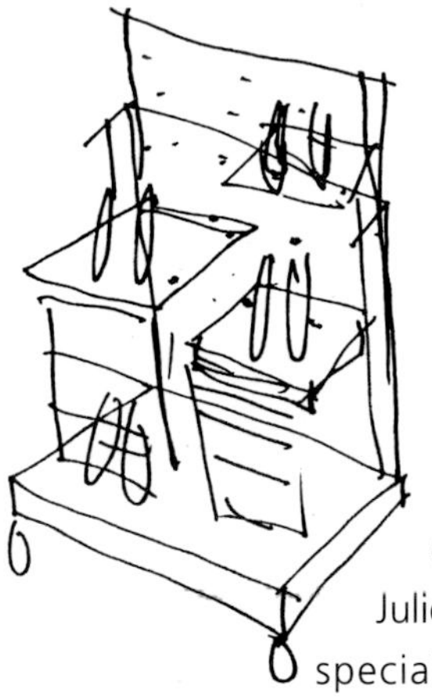

1992 the three of them started what they called, significantly, Design Ministry.

"It sums up our philosophy for the business and the way we wanted to approach design and retailing in particular. Our project teams are put together like movies," she explains. "We have four full time designers. Emma works on all the interior design aspects and Julie and David, do all the graphics. We add additional specialists as we need them". "At first I worked from home." Val recalls "Our first job was for the Bata Shoe Corporation in Paris. Their 1,500 stores throughout Europe had a bit of a communication problem. We wrote a report and made some recommendations, and helped them workout a visual merchandising and communication strategy with clearer brand identification. This became the merchandising manual to help them implement solutions in all their outlets throughout Europe".

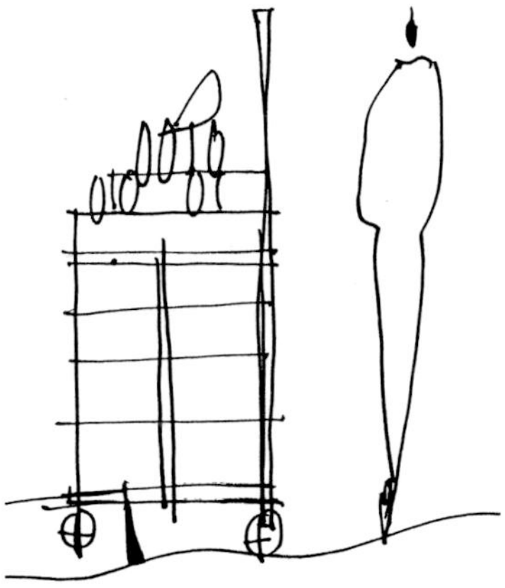

"Since we'd all been very 'hands on' in retailing we intended to apply our very practical skills to other retailers, it's as much an education process as it is a design process," Val explains.

They moved into a tiny first floor studio space in a cobbled mews beside the bustling fruit and vegetable market of London's Shepherd Bush area. "We don't have prestigious offices, but clients seem to respect the fact that our charges don't have to service high overheads. They can see what they're paying for." Says Lesley Cussé, who handles the marketing and PR for the group.

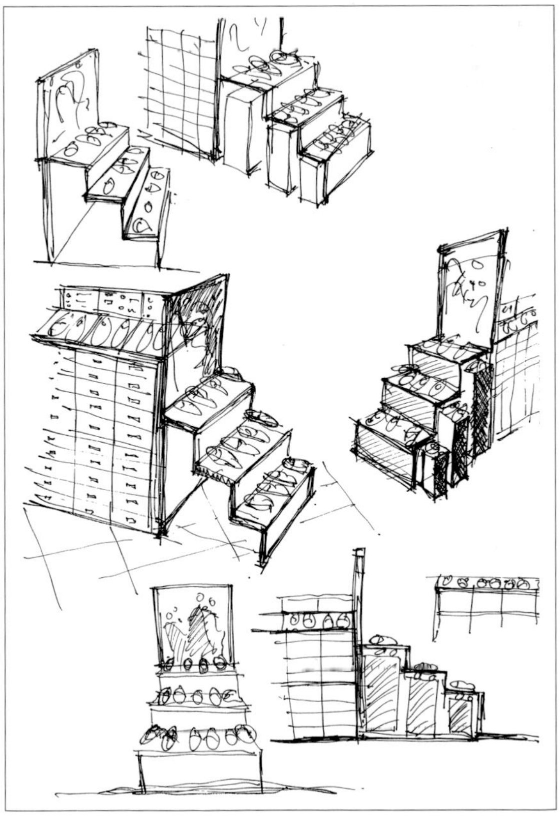

Other projects soon followed, including point-of-sale for Benetton and Sisley and packaging for Price's Candles and Acorn Marketing.

"We became frantically busy," recalls Val "and often had to work all night and all weekend. We were lucky to be working in Europe, as the recession took longer to hit there than it did in the UK".

The group also travel to America as often as they can, usually combining a visit to a trade fair with a fact-finding trip to New York or Chicago.

In 1944 the British Shoe Corporation's (B.S.C.) Deputy Managing Director, Steven Smith, contacted Design Ministry.

Val had six main questions:

Tell us what you want to achieve?

Who is your customer?

Who is your competition?

Which other companies

(not just retailers) do you like?

What don't you like?

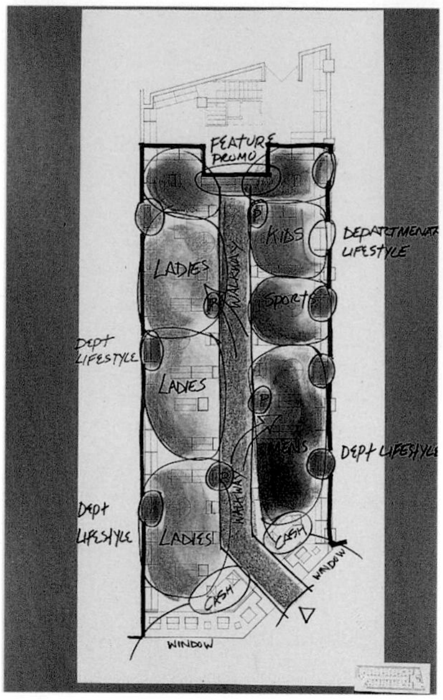

ABOVE **The first plan of the space was concerned with the layout of the product area around a wide central aisle, leading to a 'feature promotion' at the end.**

Mission

The creation of a self-service shopping environment to be used by British Shoe Corporation, to meet the following criteria:

Create a contemporary, stylish and well organised environment for assisted self-service shoe retailing, for ladies, men and children.

Provide a totally flexible merchandising format, with individual departments which can change in size to accommodate seasonal trends. The shop fit can accommodate approximately 10,000 pairs of shoes, merchandised by lifestyle.

Have a clearly defined graphics system, which acts as the vital link in establishing the style and ambience of the shop, corporate identity and also lends visual excitement and ambience.

Create a design to appeal to a wide audience – namely the mass middle market in a classless, totally approachable yet very clearly focused way, to emphasise an offer of wide choice giving exceptional value for money for all.

The key to this mission statement, is found in the words 'Assisted Self Service'. Generally shoe shops have been service orientated. If you go in for a pair of shoes, you have to wait while an assistant finishes serving the people in front of you, then wait again while he or she goes into the store room to find a pair that are your size.

At the same time, the team did not want to create a help yourself warehouse. They looked at the customer profile; a "price-driven fashion conscious, female, aged 25–30." There were plenty of research 'facts' about her, for instance, "she's called Lucy rather than Sheila!" "Value conscious, likes regular changing fashions, shops regularly, quite badly affected by recession either actually or perceptually, used to spend a lot more on fashion and shoes but arrival of family (marriage/purchase of house) has probably affected her disposable income and requirements, quite a confident individual (admits buying synthetic for a reason), probably works, will have a mixed wardrobe from expensive labels (probably a treat from when she was younger and richer) and chain store Marks & Spencer very important for clothes and probably aspires to M & S for food but probably buys from Tesco, children/family are important, understands quality and fashion, but is willing to compromise the former to achieve the latter, probably a car driver, but second hand (ie Golf), is educated (A level) but more importantly is intelligent, probably works, possibly not in such a high position as she could have achieved because of a career break/decision not to be too ambitious, lives in a 'nice' house, possibly older style but if new still has some character, sensible TV is watched rather than rubbish".

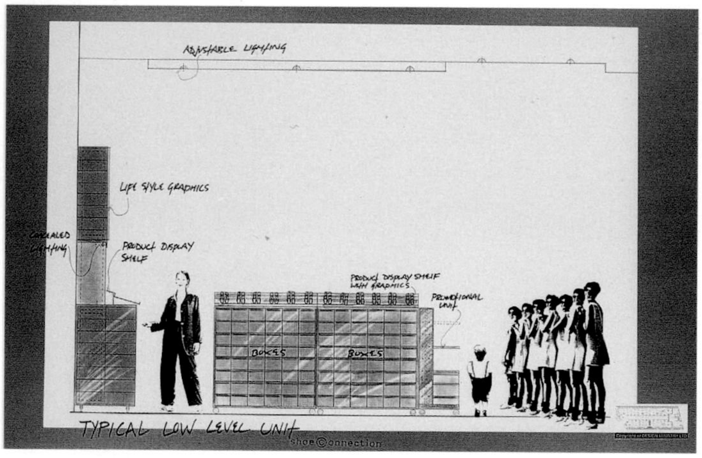

ABOVE **Low level central units carry a simple display shelf along the top. Each unit is on lockable castors.**

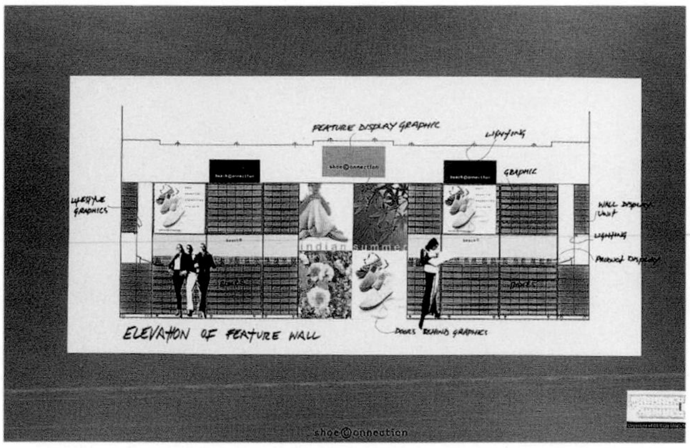

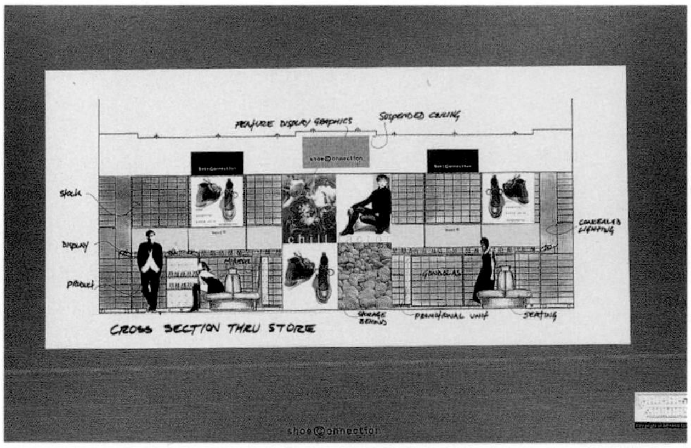

ABOVE AND ABOVE RIGHT **An elevation drawing of the feature wall at the end of the store, shows how the central space is devoted to seasonal graphics. A cross-Section through the store relates high level storage shelving to the low central elements, and shows how it is unified by the consistency of the 'pigeon hole system'.**

There was lots more. They even know what beer she drinks. In summary, the 'customer' was identified as:

Work – Supervisory/Office Worker
Education – Mainly GCSE
Dress – Safe, fairly classic, like a 35 year old
Shops – Wallis/M & S/Debenhams
Lifestyle – Stable relationship, balanced approach to leisure and work
Attitude – Feels able to make choices, looking for value

Most importantly, research showed that "As the economic recession ends, it is likely that this customer group will increase its spending on shoes and clothes, providing further medium term project potential. In addition, as you might expect, these women prefer to buy shoes for their children at the same shop".

So how does all this affect the design process? For a start, the British Shoe Corporation, who now import most of their products from abroad, already own seven other chains, many in the process of redesign, from Shoe Express (see page 168) at the lower end of the market, to the upmarket Roland Cartier (see pages 172–5).

So, positioning the brand was fundamental to the success of the contract. Val and her team also had to get to know the company, and the way shoes are packaged, shipped and stocked. Not only that, but they had only two weeks from the briefing to the first presentation of the whole concept.

Val admits she first thought of the name while driving back from the meeting. "We were very excited at the opportunity to control the entire design and communication process," explains Emma Starkin, who headed up the interior design of the store. "We wanted to prove the versatility of the design across all areas. So we did lots of big A1 presentation boards to illustrate every aspect and convince the client that the concept worked as a whole, and that every detail had been considered".

Starting with the plan, they wanted to make the shopping process as easy as possible – a wide central aisleway with all the departments off it and an enticing promotion area at the far end.

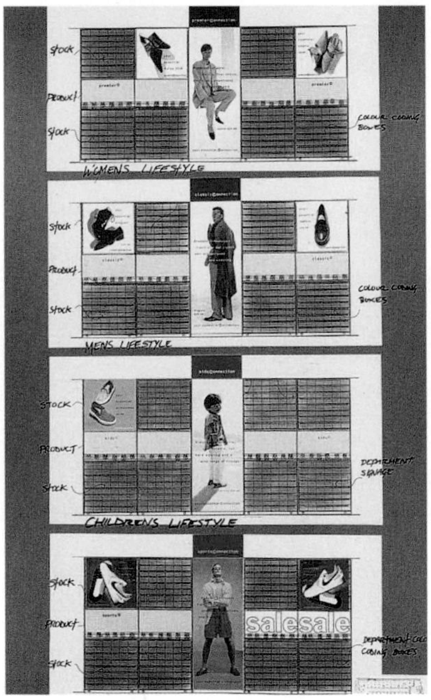

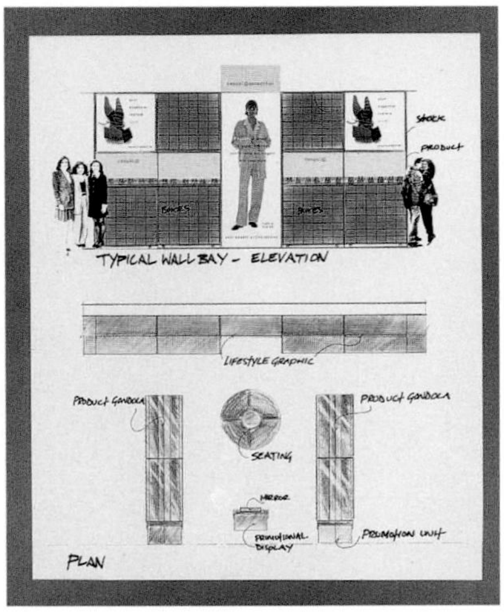

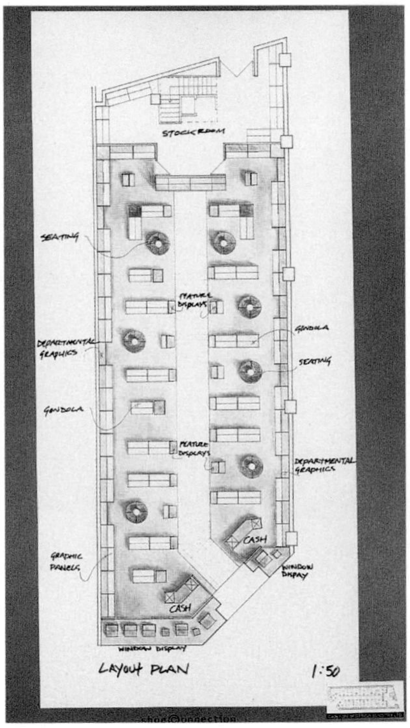

TOP **Kids Connection graphics have the unity of the primarily white background, but colour is used to relate typography to the shoe boxes.**

ABOVE **Presentation boards demonstrate the use of large photographs to highlight the lifestyle areas. Each photographic panel can be rolled across to reveal extra stock or conceal gaps.**

ABOVE **A plan of a product area shows how a wall bay for Casual Connection is related to a central seating unit and promotional display. Rugs were later added to soften the sounds of the timber floors.**

RIGHT **The finalised plan for the first store.**

If the store was going to have all the stock (10,000 pairs) out front and on display, it still had to look elegant, contemporary and simple, not too fragmented. The fixtures also had to be totally modular, all the units completely interchangeable and on lockable casters to allow for merchandising by lifestyle and seasonal adjustments.

The shoe box became the key to it all. Since it would be on view it had to look good and it had to communicate to the customer, not just the sales assistants. The size had to be standardised, so boxes could be moved around, restocked with ease, opened and closed without confusion or damage.

RIGHT **A concept board for the brown craft shoe boxes, demonstrates bold colour coding and simple typography to differentiate product groups.**

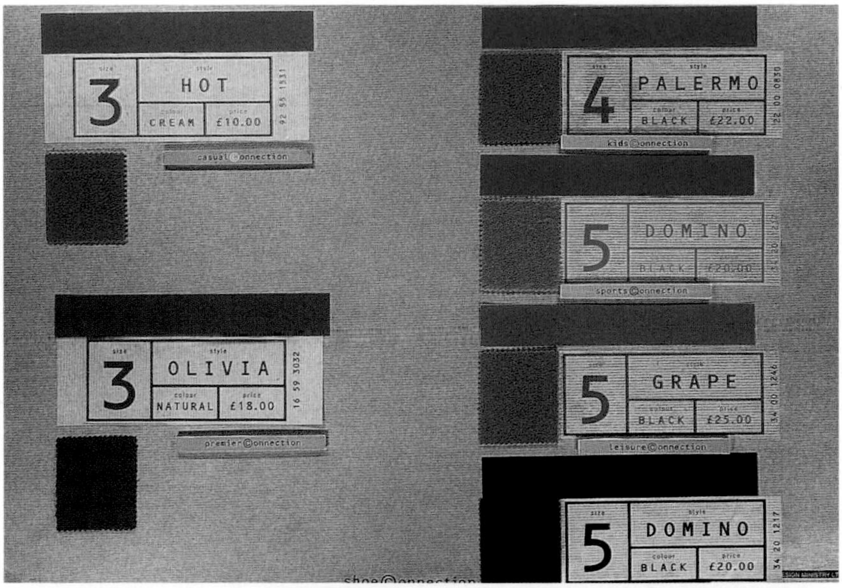

RIGHT **Considerable time and effort was spent on the shoeboxes, deciding exactly how much information was required to help both the staff and the customers. Barcodes were not included.**

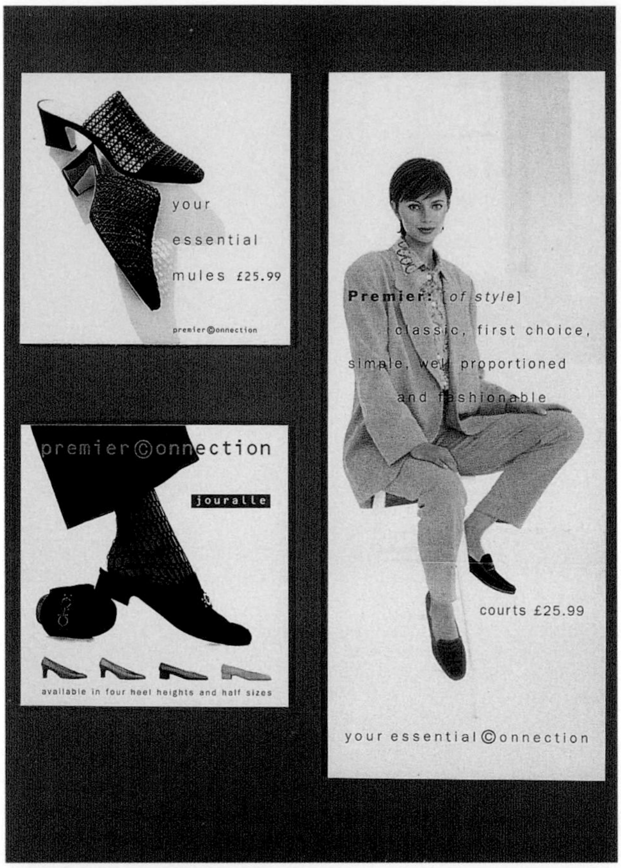

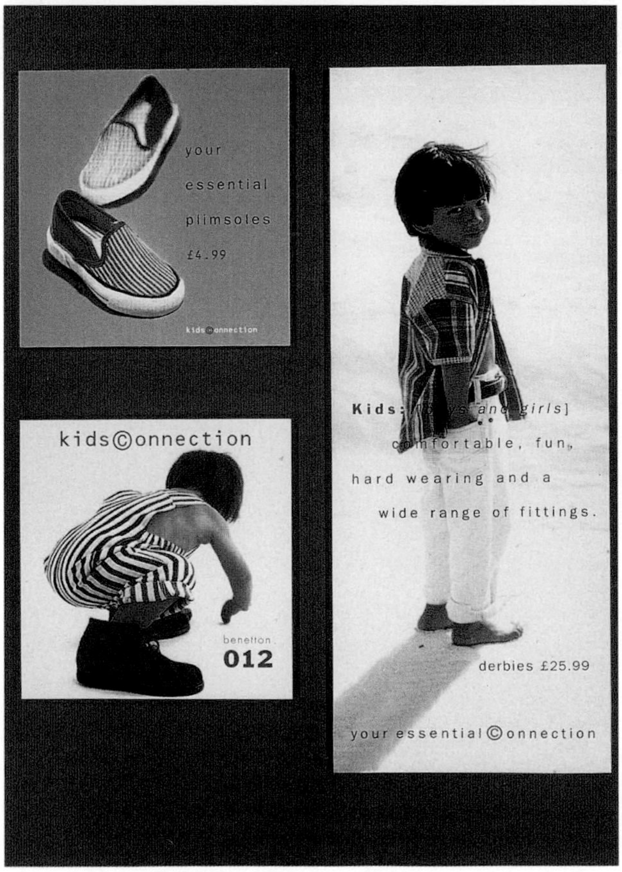

The modular photographic panels promote the relationship of fashion and footwear while the copy (set in Franklin Gothic) sells individual lines.

A modular 'pigeon hole' system had to hold boots as well as shoes, adults footwear as well as childrens, but empty spaces where products might be out of stock had to be avoided.

To divide up the space, and to highlight product areas and add a human element, large photographic prints (changed seasonally) were combined with simple information typography, but these too had to be moveable. Each area has a seat, a mirror, a rug, a promotional display (the fashion element) and a name – Premier Connection, Kids Connect, etc. Each pair of shoes is accompanied by a benefits holder displaying the key features.

The whole store is designed with the customer in mind, not just the staff, and the overall effect of the pale natural timber and elegant light background to the photographs, is cool and sophisticated.

Following approval of the concept, the designers were asked to apply the design to a prototype store, but first a section of the scheme was built in the shopfitter's workshops. There were some small modifications, in particular the size of the boxes was adjusted from the standard dimensions, so they would fit more snugly, (even though this meant a non-standard make). All the boxes are made without their end graphics, cleverly, these are applied by transparent stick-on labels, once they're packed.

TOP **The window displays were kept at low levels, so that customers could see right through into the store. It was important to demonstrate how Sale Graphics could look as good as the rest of the panels.**

ABOVE AND ABOVE LEFT **Once each of the elements was designed, the whole concept was put on computer. The designers used a mac with an In fini – d and photoshop programme, and produced two highly realistic visuals.**

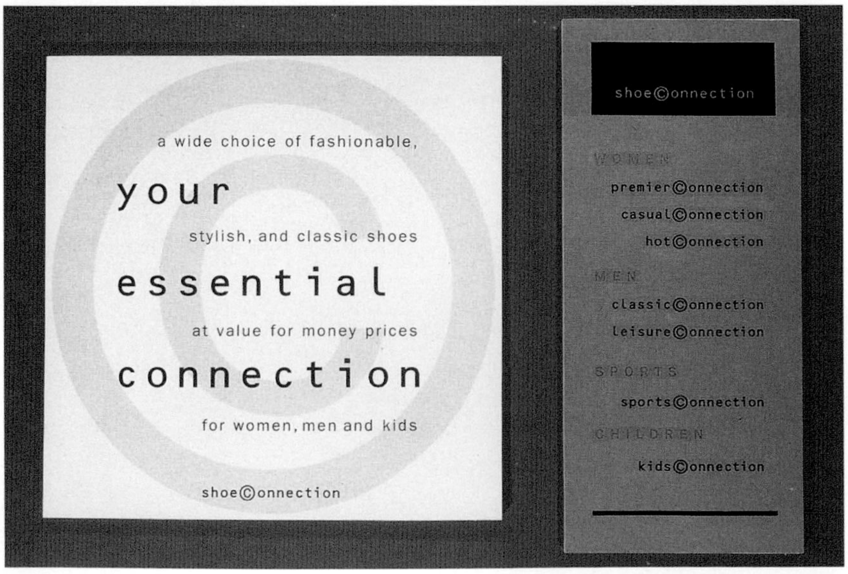

LEFT AND BELOW LEFT **Shopping bags convey the logo at maximum size but the muted use of colour has the same feel as the store. Near the doors, a large board sets out the store's mission statement, whilst smaller panels indicate the range of lifestyle areas.**

With the client's enthusiasm for the scheme, the first prototype evolved into three stores; one at Hanley, Milton Keynes and Luton, all three opened within the space of a month.

"We went up to Hanley for three days to see the first store being merchandised," recalls Emma "but then we just had to step back and watch the sales force take over".

Now the team have turned their attention to two high street sites to apply the design to smaller spaces. Once it's seen that it is achieving the required sales figures, 30 more will be 'rolled out' over the next six months with the aim of increasing this to 100 or 150.

In the meantime, what about other design work? Modestly, Val confesses that "We wouldn't say no to another shoe store client, but at the moment we're designing a hi-fi and video store, and tomorrow we're going to Milan to talk to a possible new client." Modesty seems to underscore much of their approach to the business but Val adds, "Looking at Shoe Connection now it's all finished, I don't think there's anything we'd do differently".

ABOVE **Boards in the presentation indicated the range and variety that the seasonal promotions could achieve. The designers provide on-going input into the production of these panels.**

Shoe Connection

COUNTRY OF ORIGIN: United Kingdom

DESIGNER: Design Ministry, London, England

DATE: 1995

TYPE OF IDENTITY IMPLEMENTATION: Complete Identity

TARGET AUDIENCE: All ages

CLIENT'S BRIEF: To create a totally new, modern and competitive shoe store for the British Shoe Corporation (B.S.C.). A shoe store to revolutionise Britain's high streets

DESIGN RATIONALE: Design Ministry was given total creative control over the store and everything in it. Many of the B.S.C's existing stores were not suitable for conversion so these were sold and appropriate sites chosen for Shoe Connection. This case study illustrates a radical approach and excellent application of graphics in high street retail

(continued on pp 18-21)

shoe©onnection
premier©onnection
classic©onnection
self service shoes
boat shoes £25

shoe©onnection
shoe©onnection
WOMEN
premier©onnection
casual©onnection
MEN
classic©onnection
leisure©onnection
SPORTS
sports©onnection
CHILDREN
kids©onnection

premier©onnection
your
essential
courts
£18
shoe©onnection

FIRE EXIT
spring blossoms

classic©onnection
leisure©onnection
sports©onnection
shoe©onnection
Welcome to Shoe Connection

premier©onnection
leisure©onnection
sports©onnection
shoe©onnection

your
essential
boots £25
your
essential
connection
shoe©onnection
Welcome to Shoe Connection.
Please feel free to browse and try on your shoes at your leisure. If you need assistance - we will be pleased to help you.
The shoes
are arranged in order of size directly beneath the display pair. Please replace any shoes that you do not wish to purchase, for the convenience of other customers.
If you don't see your size please ask.
A customer comments book
is situated at the cash desk, and we welcome your comments to help us to help you better.
Thank you for shopping at Shoe Connection
onnection

sports©onnection
leisure©onnection
classic©onnection
shoe©onnection
sports©onnection
fitness
shoes £15

your essential
classic
loafers
£20
casual©onnection
casual©

GIFTS & HOME ACCESSORIES

1

Capi Live

COUNTRY OF ORIGIN: The Netherlands

DESIGNER: Carole van Bekkum, André Schopman/Keja Donia, Amsterdam, The Netherlands

DATE: 1994 April

TYPE OF IDENTITY IMPLEMENTATION: Complete identity

TARGET AUDIENCE: Photography enthusiasts and professionals

CLIENT'S BRIEF: To bring our chain of photography specialist stores up to date with market conditions, retaining a quality image: outstanding, different and distinctive

DESIGN RATIONALE: The traditional approach to photography uses technique as a starting point. Capi Live takes the emotion of the image as the central point of departure; the things that one registers in life are important. The product groups are clustered in an active and human way, the result is inspired and surprising

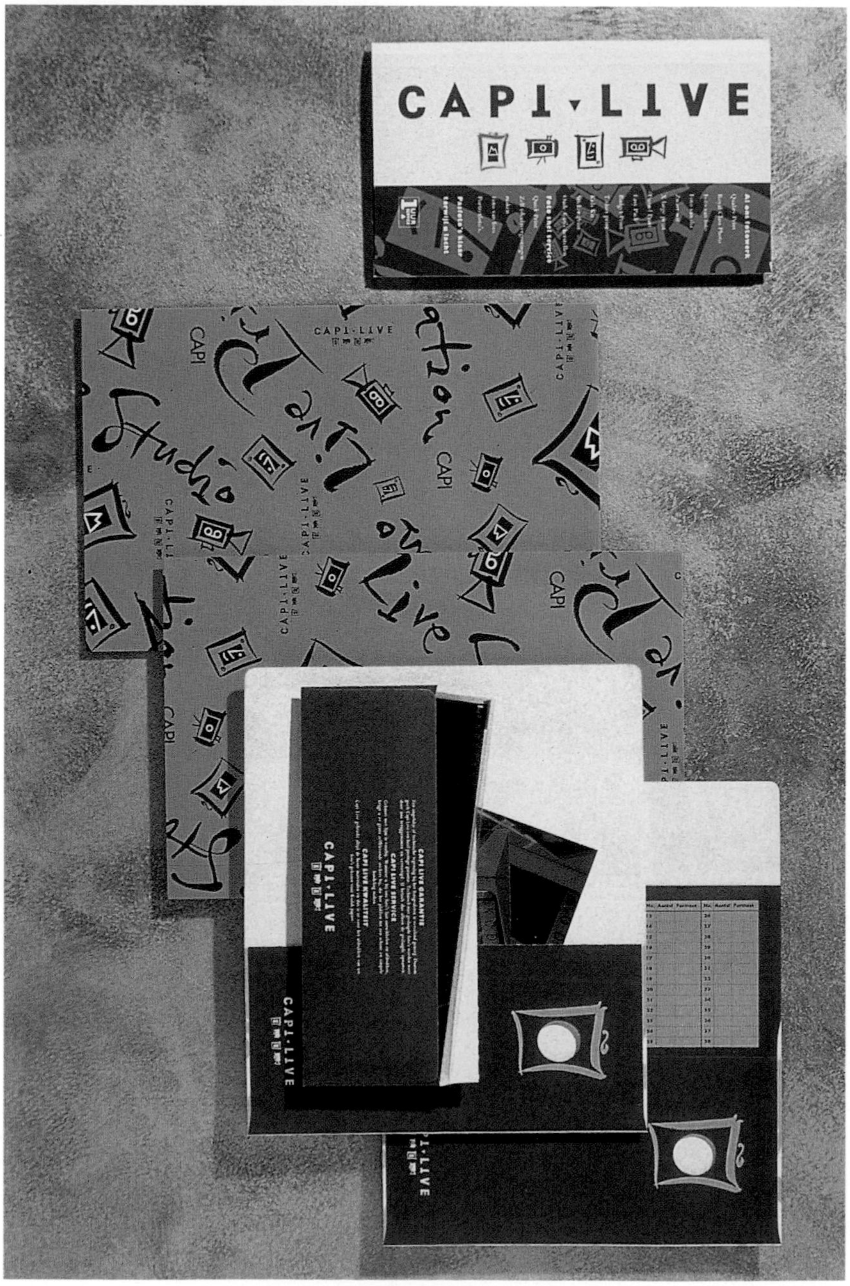

Flitsend type
voor een schijntje.

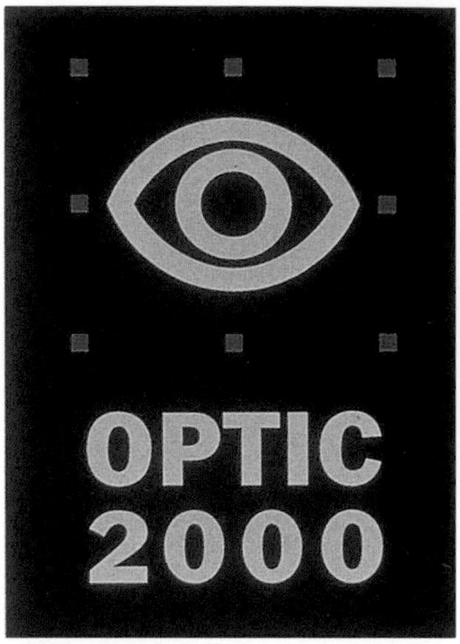

Optic 2000

COUNTRY OF ORIGIN: France

DESIGNER: Joël Desgrippes/Desgrippes & Associés, Paris, France

DATE: 1994

TYPE OF IDENTITY IMPLEMENTATION: Corporate identity, signs, frontage, furniture and fittings of the shops

TARGET AUDIENCE: Optic 2000's customers

CLIENT'S BRIEF: To create a positioning that expresses the complementary qualities of the optician's work: not only medical, technical and pragmatic know-how but also psychological abilities and an aesthetic sensitiveness

DESIGN RATIONALE: A new identity was created to make an impact bringing Optic 2000 in line with modern needs. It takes into account the consumers' expectations for a brighter and warmer space and for better visualisation of the products

OPTIC 2000
OPTIC
2000
OPTIC
2000

Ordning & Reda Paper and Design UK Ltd

COUNTRY OF ORIGIN: Sweden

DESIGNER: Carina Ahnberg/Ordning & Reda Paper and Design, Sweden

DATE: 1982 Sweden, 1994 November London

TYPE OF IDENTITY IMPLEMENTATION: Complete identity

TARGET AUDIENCE: Women aged between 20–50 years

CLIENT'S BRIEF: To create a new positioning for Ordning & Reda. Using colour and design to inspire the individual at home and in the office

DESIGN RATIONALE: A modern and unique design was developed which combines high quality and functionality, as well as an environmentally friendly manufacturing process

ORDNING & REDA

ORDNING & REDA

Squawk!

COUNTRY OF ORIGIN: United Kingdom

DESIGNER: Michael Matenczuk and Steve Lascelles

DATE: 1994 June

TYPE OF IDENTITY IMPLEMENTATION: Shop sign, bags, stationery, own product branding

TARGET AUDIENCE: Local domestic customers and foreign trade

CLIENT'S BRIEF: A strong image was required to reflect the eclectic nature of the merchandise on sale. A mixture of old and modern furniture, artifacts and giftware

DESIGN RATIONALE: The bird and mirror image was initially conceived to represent the company's original business of producing unusual mirrors. When the business evolved to include selling unusual furniture and artifacts, the image still remained relevant – the name SQUAWK! having connotations of an amused or surprised exclamation. The image is now being simplified by removing the mirror from the bird

Squawk!
51 TOPSFIELD PARADE
TOTTENHAM LANE
LONDON N8
0181 245 3147

MXYPLYZYK
MXYPLYZYK
MXYPLYZY

MXYPLYZYK

MXYPLYZYK

MXYPLYZYK

COUNTRY OF ORIGIN: America
DESIGNER: Gail Rigelhaupt
DATE: 1992 October
TYPE OF IDENTITY IMPLEMENTATION: Logo
TARGET AUDIENCE: General public
CLIENT'S BRIEF: To take the name MXYPLYZYK (which means nothing) and make it interesting, graphic, and memorable. (Remembering how to spell it or pronounce it was secondary)
DESIGN RATIONALE: The name was stretched to the max to emphasize it. Also a modern and clean typeface was chosen to eliminate any historical references, for example to the Greek alphabet
ADDITIONAL CREDITS: Brian Fingeret (shopping bag label) Lauren Caldivell (New Designers invitation)
PHOTOGRAPHER: Stephanie Berger

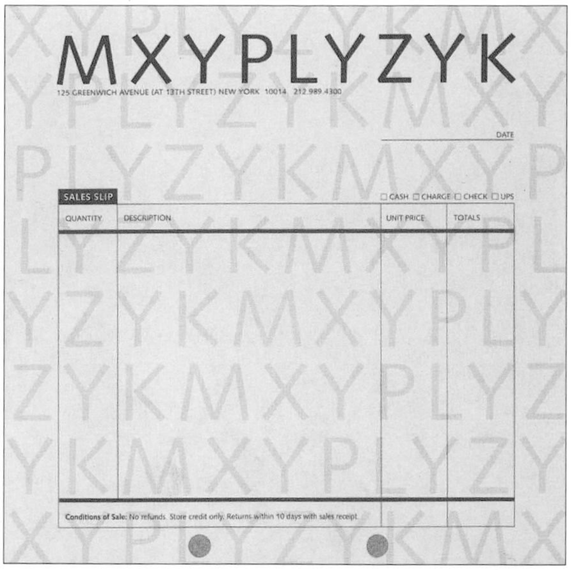

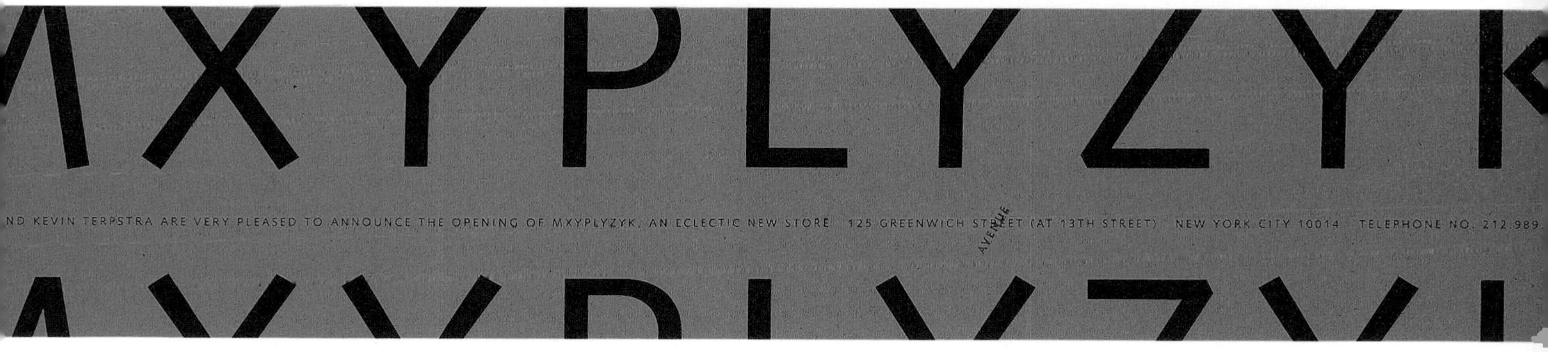

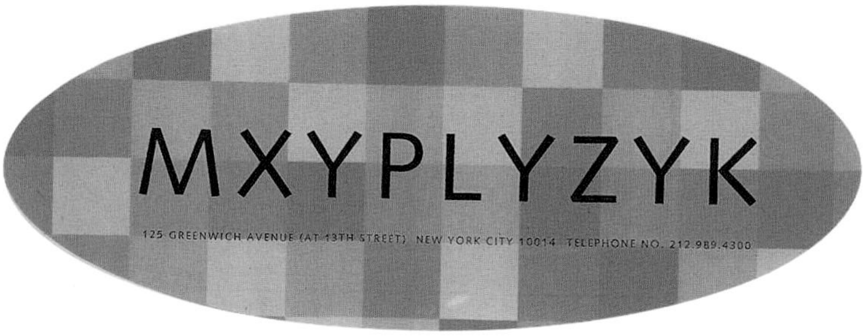

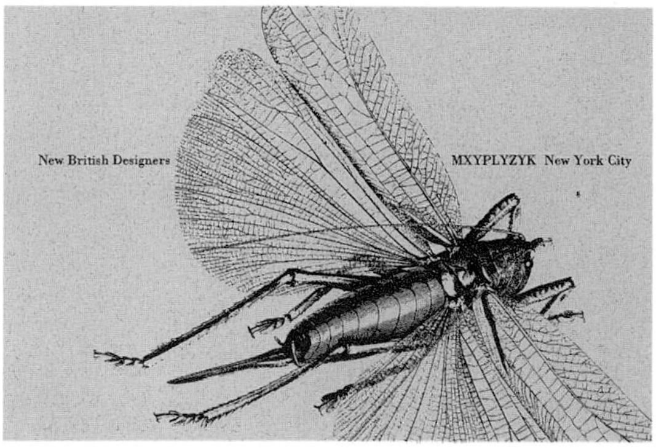

HEAL'S

Heal's

COUNTRY OF ORIGIN: United Kingdom

DESIGNER: Mary Lewis/Lewis Moberly, London, England

DATE: 1991

TYPE OF IDENTITY IMPLEMENTATION: Stationery, carrier bags, livery, packaging

TARGET AUDIENCE: General public

CLIENT'S BRIEF: The Company aimed to re-establish its individuality and distinctive character, and its unique reputation for exclusive, well-designed crafted furniture and household products

DESIGN RATIONALE: The new logo aims to be timeless and distinctive and to stand apart from the overt 'designer' logos of previous years. The letterforms are hand drawn with an inlaid detail inspired by the use of inlay on so many of Heal's most distinctive pieces. It is designed to support the product, not to compete with or overwhelm it

HEAL'S

HEAL'S

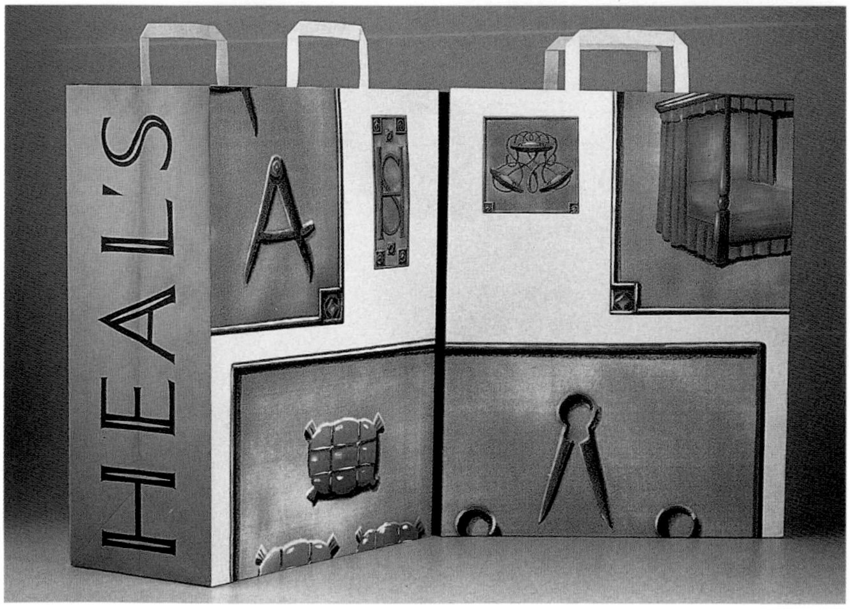
HEAL'S

MIKISSIME

Mikissimes Optical

COUNTRY OF ORIGIN: France

DESIGNER: Carré Noir, Paris, France

DATE: 1994

TYPE OF IDENTITY IMPLEMENTATION: Packaging, exterior and interior design, signage, logo

TARGET AUDIENCE: General public

CLIENT'S BRIEF: To launch the first Paris Miki, a Japanese optician, in France

DESIGN RATIONALE: The architectural concept was created by Carré Noir using advanced technology with an aesthetic feel and refinement. A mix of materials were used including Canadian sycamore and stone walls. A starlit sky ceiling envelops the whole high-tech environment

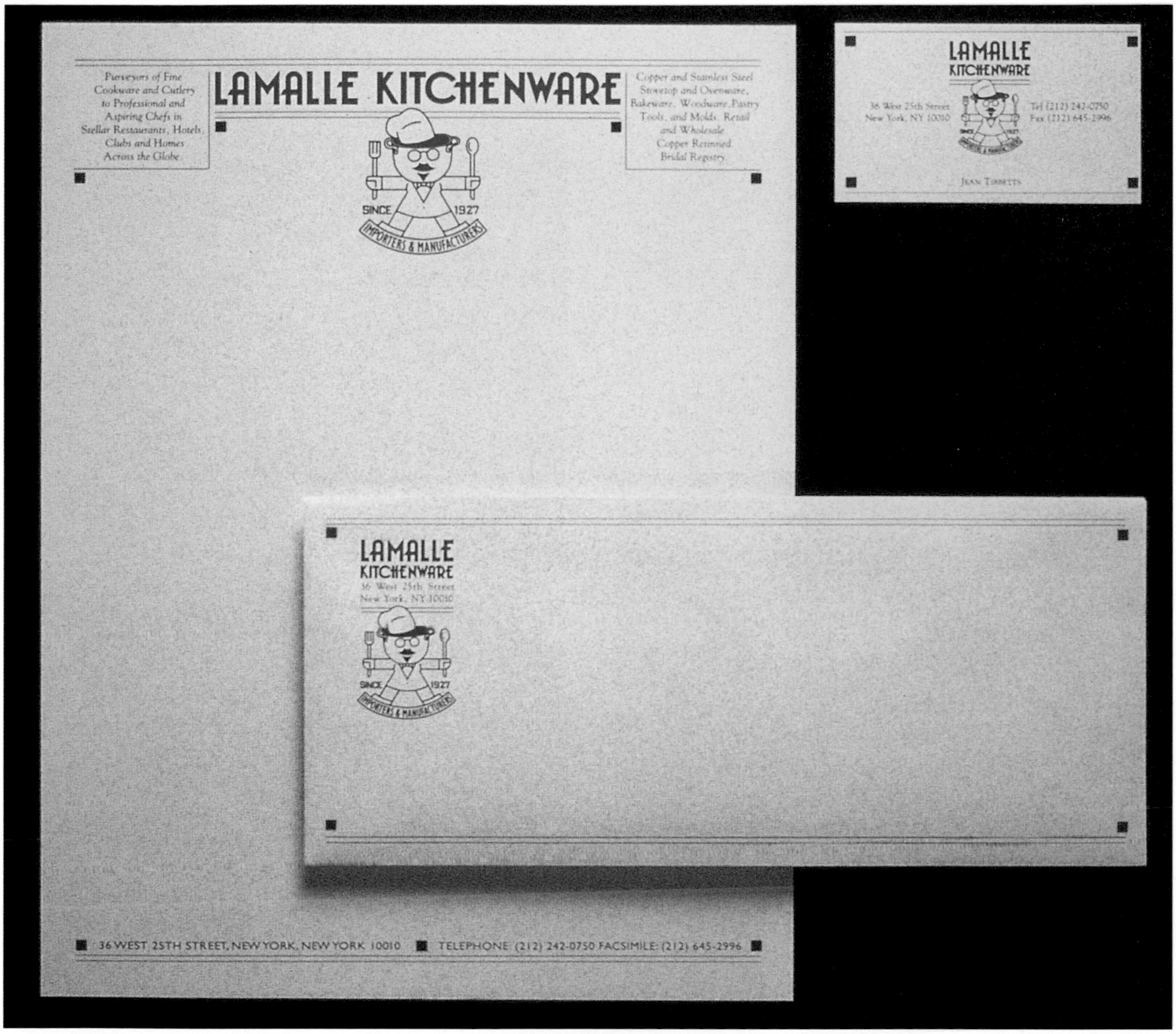

Lamalle Kitchenware

COUNTRY OF ORIGIN: America

DESIGNER: Seymour Chwast/The Pushpin Group Inc., New York, USA

DATE: 1994

TYPE OF IDENTITY IMPLEMENTATION: Stationery and T-shirts

TARGET AUDIENCE: General public

CLIENT'S BRIEF: We were asked to provide a mark and logo that would reflect the quality and tradition of a half-century old firm, importing and selling top-of-the-range kitchen equipment. The mark and logo had to be used in a variety of sizes and applications

DESIGN RATIONALE: This mark and the use of a character was designed to look as If It was the original. A retailer this old would be perceived to be a purveyor of quality merchandise. The bold deco identification contrasts with the thin line mark

Jerry's Home Store

COUNTRY OF ORIGIN: United Kingdom

DESIGNER: Davies/Baron, London, England

DATE: 1993

TYPE OF IDENTITY IMPLEMENTATION: Fascia, internal signage, carrier bags, packaging

TARGET AUDIENCE: People who enjoy entertaining at home

CLIENT'S BRIEF: To create a simple and stylish American-style environment. To fit out the store at minimum cost

DESIGN RATIONALE: Davies/Baron developed the name, identity and full interior scheme. This is made up of duck boarding around the walls, a hundred year old pine floor and an elegant timber staircase. The concept emulates the American stores of this nature such as Crate & Barrel

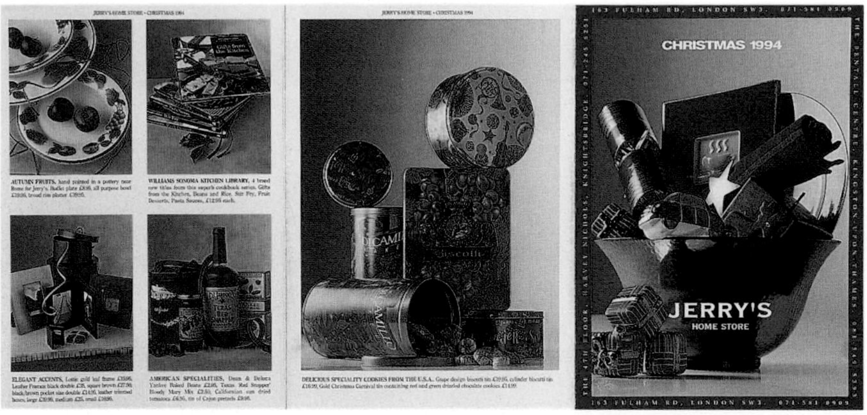
CHRISTMAS 1994
JERRY'S
HOME STORE

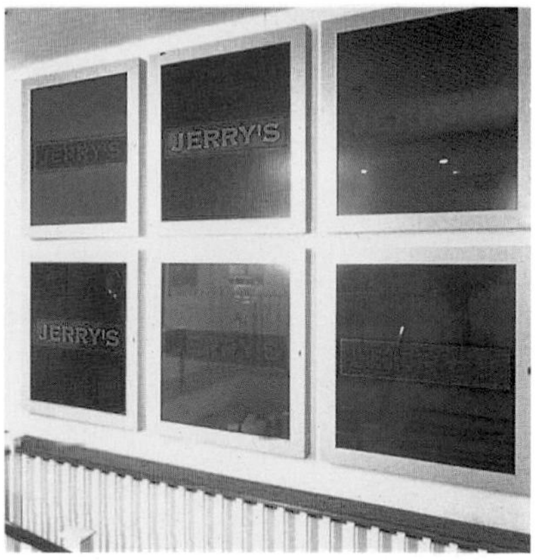
JERRY'S

JERRY'S
HOME STORE

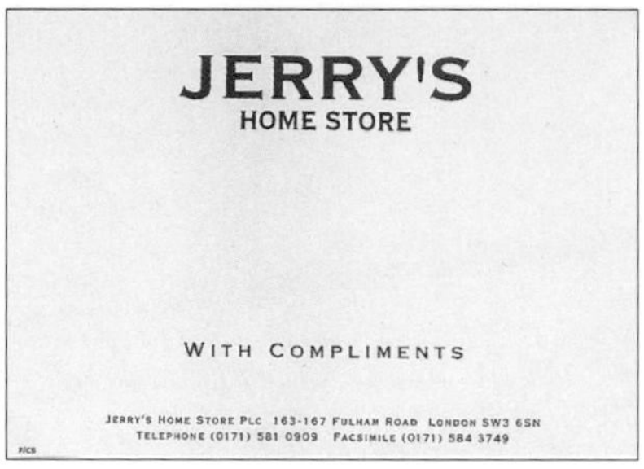
JERRY'S
HOME STORE
WITH COMPLIMENTS
JERRY'S HOME STORE PLC 163-167 FULHAM ROAD LONDON SW3 6SN
TELEPHONE (0171) 581 0909 FACSIMILE (0171) 584 3749

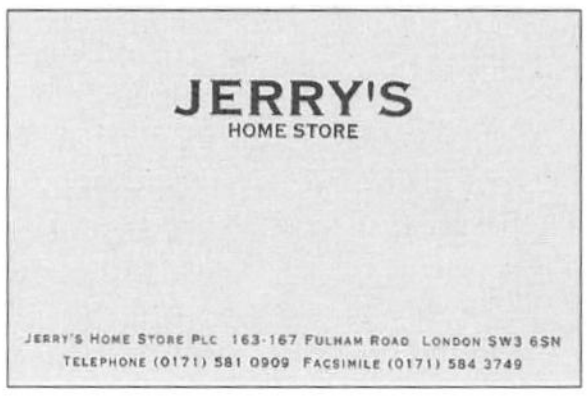
JERRY'S
HOME STORE
JERRY'S HOME STORE PLC 163-167 FULHAM ROAD LONDON SW3 6SN
TELEPHONE (0171) 581 0909 FACSIMILE (0171) 584 3749

JERRY'S
HOME STORE

JERRY'S
WEDDING LIST

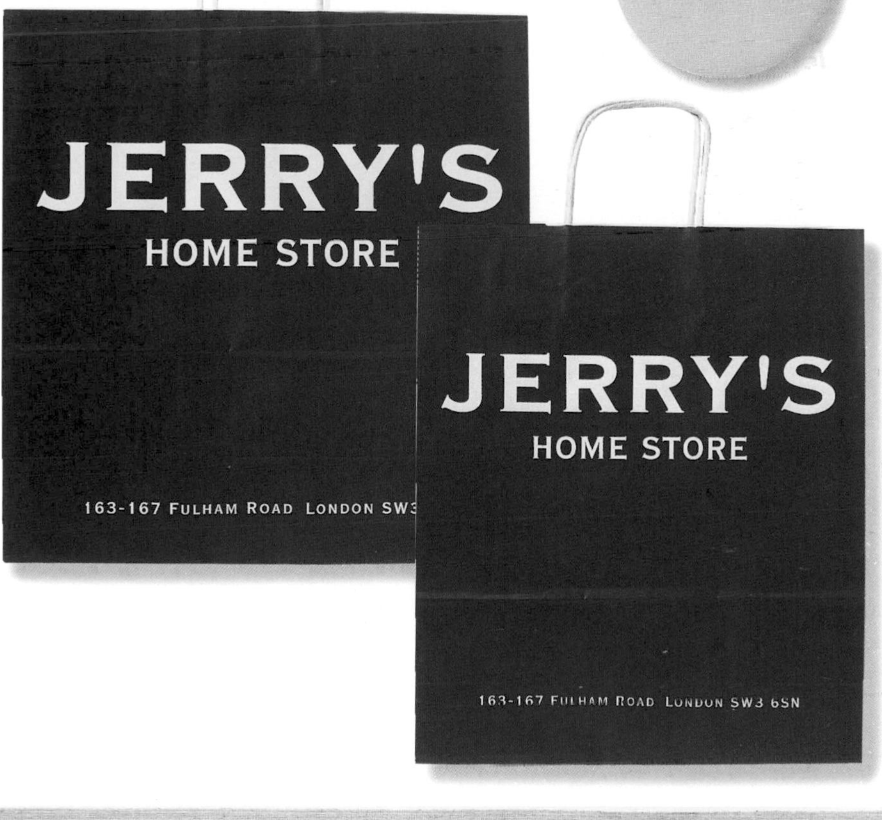
JERRY'S
HOME STORE
163-167 FULHAM ROAD LONDON SW3
JERRY'S
HOME STORE
163-167 FULHAM ROAD LONDON SW3 6SN

• JERRY'S • JERRY'S • JERRY'S • JERRY'S •

Castelbajac

COUNTRY OF ORIGIN: France
DESIGNER: Marc Boisseuil
DATE: 1993
TYPE OF IDENTITY IMPLEMENTATION: Complete identity
TARGET AUDIENCE: General public
CLIENT'S BRIEF: To create a gallery-type atmosphere in which to display the merchandise so encouraging browsing and appreciation of the items on sale
DESIGN RATIONALE: A peaceful and serene calm pervades the shop due to the displays designed from the merchandise. A plethora of colours dance around the light and airy interior to anticipate a feeling of fun and excitement. Shopping should always be a pleasure not a chore

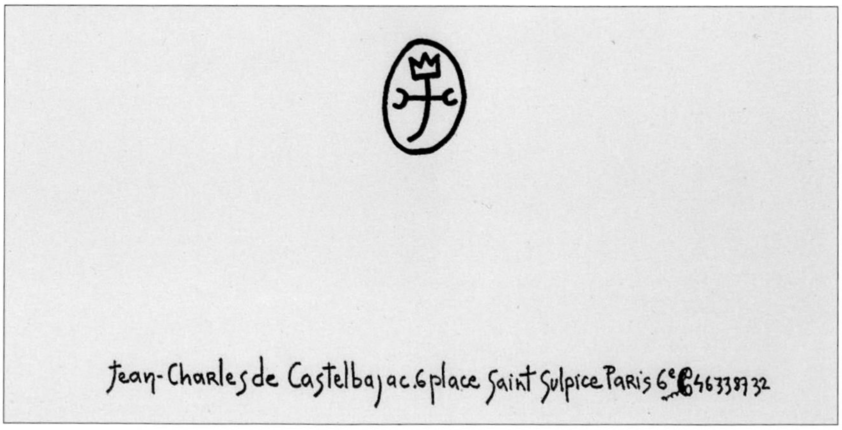

Intérieurs

COUNTRY OF ORIGIN: America
DESIGNER: Laurence Kriegel
DATE: 1993
TYPE OF IDENTITY IMPLEMENTATION: Stationery, internal signage, logo
TARGET AUDIENCE: Those sensitive to quality, shape, colour, and ambience
CLIENT'S BRIEF: To attract a better class of well-travelled, design conscious clientele
DESIGN RATIONALE: Our 'mis en scene' in the store is a balance between modern and antique. The aim of the decor is to present the merchandise in an elegant way whilst remaining unpretentious

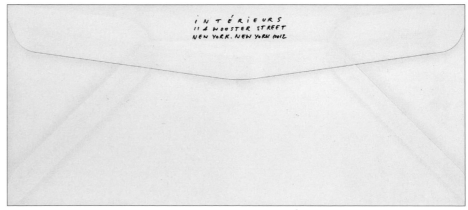

intérieurs

114 WOOSTER STREET

NEW YORK . NEW YORK 10012

TEL (212) 343_0800

FAX (212) 343_1229

intérieurs

LAURENCE KRIEGEL

114 WOOSTER STREET

NEW YORK . NEW YORK 10012

TEL (212) 343_2201

FAX (212) 343_1229

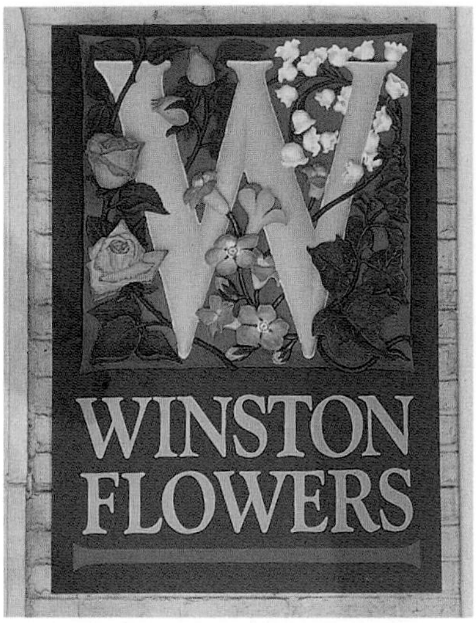

Winston Flowers

COUNTRY OF ORIGIN: USA
DESIGNER: Tricia McMahon/Hill, Holiday, Connors Cosmopulos Inc., Boston, Massachusetts, USA
DATE: 1993
TYPE OF IDENTITY IMPLEMENTATION: Store signage, stationery, sweatshirts, T-shirts, gift cards, wrapping paper
TARGET AUDIENCE: General public and corporate accounts
CLIENT'S BRIEF: To redesign the logo and identity to serve a clientèle which demands the very best in quality whilst retaining the traditional atmosphere
DESIGN RATIONALE: The store is a chain of family-owned and operated flower stores with a 45 year tradition of quality products and personalised service. The corporate identity system combines the look of fine engraving with a classic turn of the century illustration style to create a truly elegant mark that conveys Winston's old world attitudes towards quality, customer service and attention to detail
PHOTOGRAPHS: Mike Ryan and Craig Orsini
ILLUSTRATOR Bruce Hutchinson
SIGNMAKER: Artistic Sign and Carving

WINSTON FLOWERS
131 Newbury Street
The Mall at Chestnut Hill
WINSTON FLOWERS
131 Newbury Street • 569 Boylston Street
The Mall at Chestnut Hill
31 Central Street, Wellesley
P.O. Box 933 • Boston, Massachusetts 02117

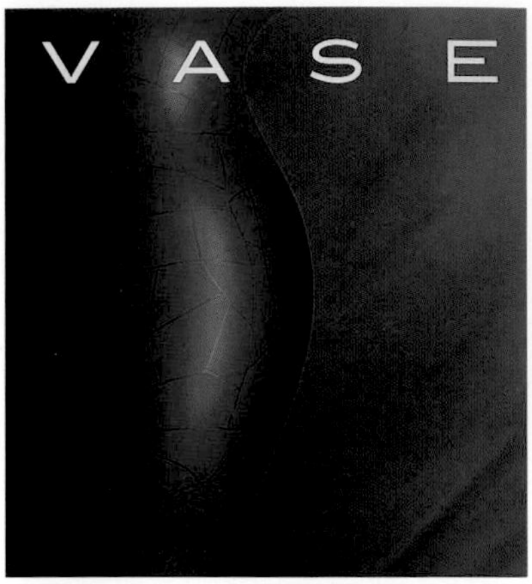

Vase

COUNTRY OF ORIGIN: United Kingdom

DESIGNER: Design House, London, England

DATE: 1989–1990

TYPE OF IDENTITY IMPLEMENTATION: Fascia, internal signage, store layout, product adjacencies, merchandising, fixtures, point-of-sale, signage, printed communications

TARGET AUDIENCE: Principally women who take an interest in the appearance of their homes – likely to be readers of Elle Decoration, Next

CLIENT'S BRIEF: To successfully establish an identity, shop design and printed communications for a new retail floristry business with a unique, differentiated product and service offer. The dominant theme was to be 'flowers for modern living' – to communicate that flowers should become a regular purchase and an integral part of daily living, rather than a one-off, 'guilt-motivated' purchase

DESIGN RATIONALE: The colours of the cornflower; saturated green and blue, were used for the identity and throughout the store. The generation of the name, 'Vase', was derived from the intention to incorporate vases of flowers into everyday living – purchasing flowers for *your* vase, rather than for someone else's

VASE
flowers for modern living
V A S E
V A S E
flowers for modern living
V A S E
flowers for modern living

VASE
flowers for modern living

Chelsea Lighting Design Ltd

COUNTRY OF ORIGIN: United Kingdom

DESIGNER: Martin Devlin, Brigid McMullen/The Workroom, London, England

DATE: 1991 April

TYPE OF IDENTITY IMPLEMENTATION: Bags, stationery

TARGET AUDIENCE: Retail public, architects, specifiers, designers, contractors

CLIENT'S BRIEF: To create an image that is capable of presenting the selling of 'light' to the individual shopper and professional groups alike. The image should be clear and simple with an element of wit and imagination

DESIGN RATIONALE: Chelsea Lighting Design was formed to offer both consultancy services and a supply capability. The Chelsea showroom is both a demonstration area for clients and a retail facility. A fundamental objective of the design is to identify the creative contribution and enjoyment of 'light' and lighting within this context

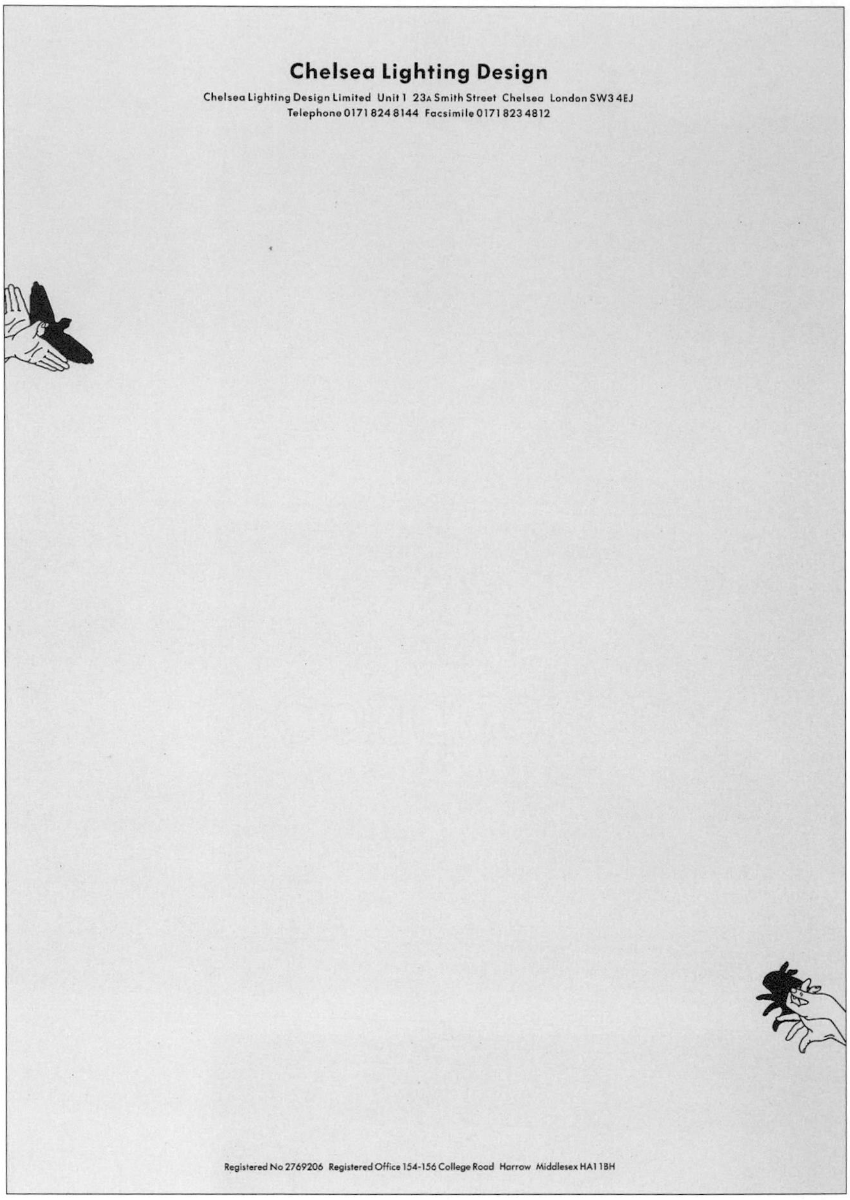

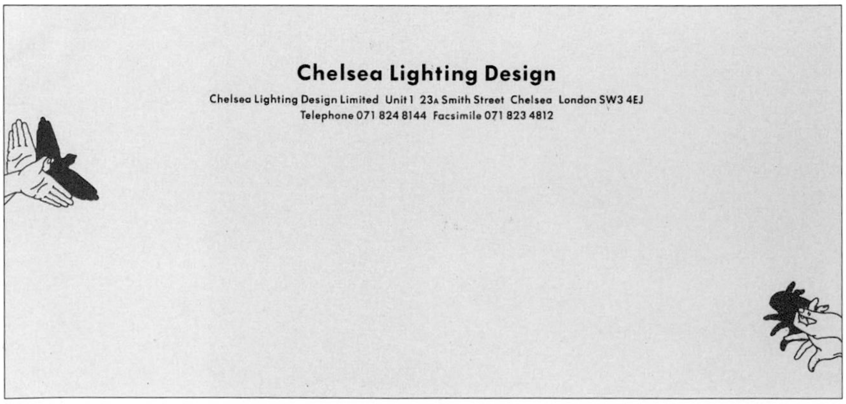

Chelsea Lighting Design
Lighting to effect

Chelsea Lighting Design
wish you a very merry Christmas and a prosperous New Year

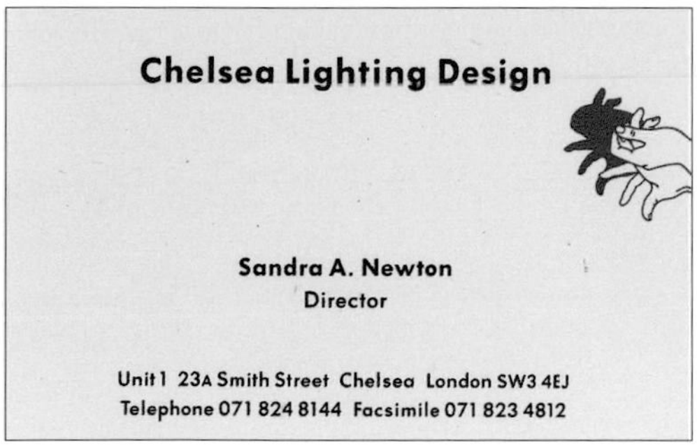
Chelsea Lighting Design
Sandra A. Newton
Director
Unit 1 23A Smith Street Chelsea London SW3 4EJ
Telephone 071 824 8144 Facsimile 071 823 4812

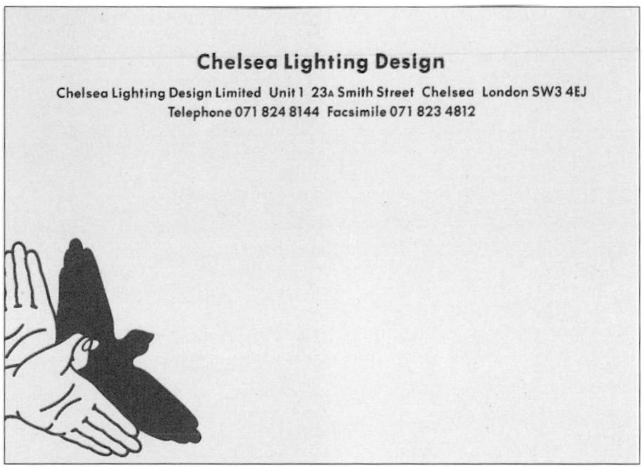
Chelsea Lighting Design
Chelsea Lighting Design Limited Unit 1 23A Smith Street Chelsea London SW3 4EJ
Telephone 071 824 8144 Facsimile 071 823 4812

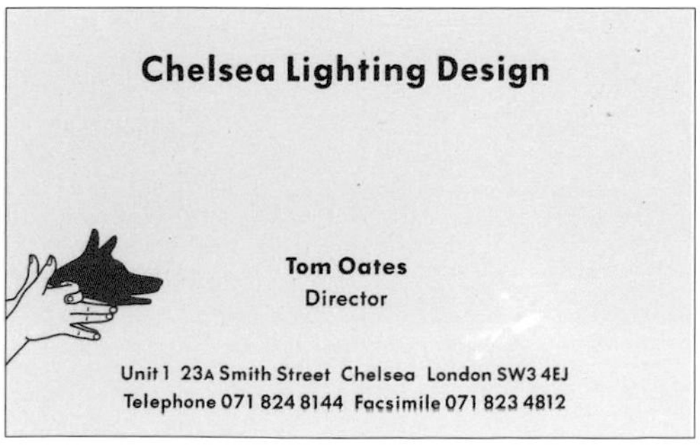
Chelsea Lighting Design
Tom Oates
Director
Unit 1 23A Smith Street Chelsea London SW3 4EJ
Telephone 071 824 8144 Facsimile 071 823 4812

B. Dalton Bookseller

COUNTRY OF ORIGIN: America
DESIGNER: Pam Bliss, Lisa Bollman, Theresa Henrekin, Jane McNeely/AIA and Jim Keane, Idie McGinty, Tim McGinty/Kiku Obata & Company, Missouri, USA
DATE: 1994
TYPE OF IDENTITY IMPLEMENTATION: All elements
TARGET AUDIENCE: Mall shoppers
CLIENT'S BRIEF: To an entertaining experience. To project the image of being the 'USA Today' of book stores, to be universally appealing, full of new ideas and information whilst remaining easy to access
DESIGN RATIONALE: In the first 30ft of the store, referred to as the 'infocore', the best sellers and newest books are displayed. A seating area invites shoppers to 'enjoy a book'. There is a special children's section. Dramatic lighting, colourful signage and the new logo were all designed as mobile fixtures to allow for constant change. The special merchandising fixtures draw the customer through the store
FIXTURES: The Butler Group, Design Fabricators, RDA, Inc., USA
PHOTOGRAPHER: Cheryl Pendelton
SIGNAGE FABRICATORS: Midtown Neon and Engraving Unlimited, USA

KID'S BOOKS
Picture Books
Non-Fiction
Classics
Series
Bookapotamus
AT HOME

B.DALTON
KID'S BOOKS
Give the perfect gift anytime...
give a B.Dalton gift certificate

NEWSSTAND
charming
weave
style
spicy
luxurious

Enjoy a Book
Enjoy a Book
TRUE CRIME
BIOGRAPHY
GREAT BOOKS AT GREAT PRICES

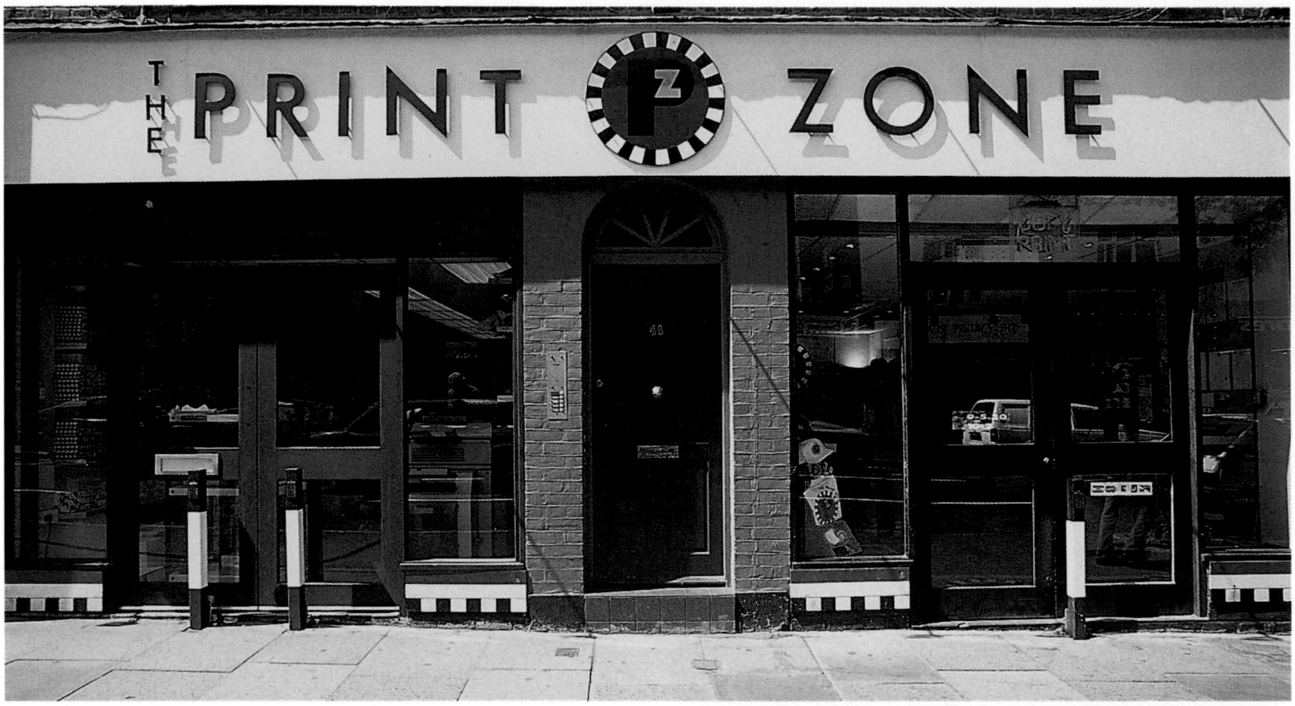

The Print Zone

COUNTRY OF ORIGIN: United Kingdom
DESIGNER: Steve Taylor/Steve Taylor & Associates, London, England
DATE: 1993 November
TYPE OF IDENTITY IMPLEMENTATION: Signage, shop front, stationery, promotional literature, uniforms, newsletter
TARGET AUDIENCE: Local business market
CLIENT'S BRIEF: To produce a highly visual and colourful logo that would indicate a one stop graphic communication. The design had to lift what could be seen as a franchised print shop to that of a digital printing service bureau. The aim also was to obtain a design suitable for any location
DESIGN RATIONALE: A bold design is used, black lettering on a white background, a layer of black and white encircles a solid blue containing the letters 'P' and 'Z'. These graphics reinforce the type of work undertaken
DESIGN MANAGER: Mike Barton-Harvey

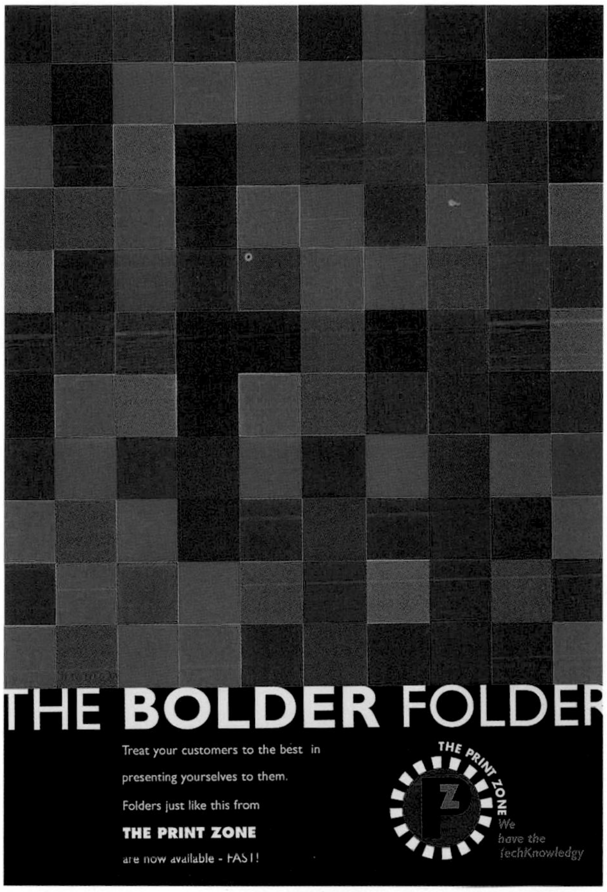

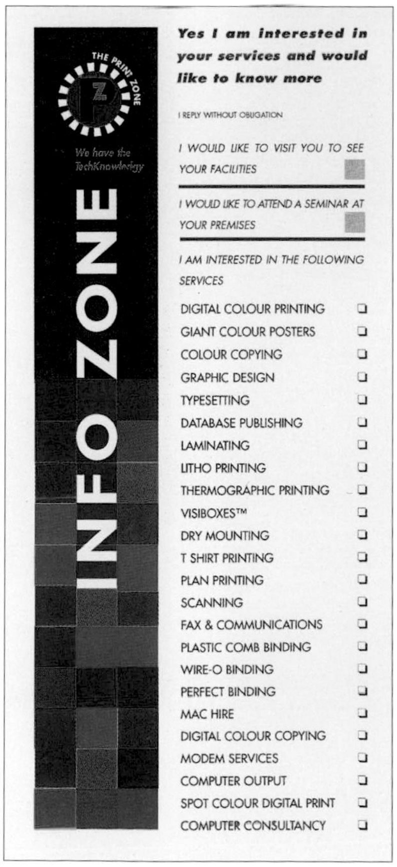
THE PRINT ZONE
We have the TechKnowledgy
INFO ZONE

Yes I am interested in your services and would like to know more

I REPLY WITHOUT OBLIGATION

I WOULD LIKE TO VISIT YOU TO SEE YOUR FACILITIES

I WOULD LIKE TO ATTEND A SEMINAR AT YOUR PREMISES

I AM INTERESTED IN THE FOLLOWING SERVICES

- DIGITAL COLOUR PRINTING ❑
- GIANT COLOUR POSTERS ❑
- COLOUR COPYING ❑
- GRAPHIC DESIGN ❑
- TYPESETTING ❑
- DATABASE PUBLISHING ❑
- LAMINATING ❑
- LITHO PRINTING ❑
- THERMOGRAPHIC PRINTING ❑
- VISIBOXES™ ❑
- DRY MOUNTING ❑
- T SHIRT PRINTING ❑
- PLAN PRINTING ❑
- SCANNING ❑
- FAX & COMMUNICATIONS ❑
- PLASTIC COMB BINDING ❑
- WIRE-O BINDING ❑
- PERFECT BINDING ❑
- MAC HIRE ❑
- DIGITAL COLOUR COPYING ❑
- MODEM SERVICES ❑
- COMPUTER OUTPUT ❑
- SPOT COLOUR DIGITAL PRINT ❑
- COMPUTER CONSULTANCY ❑

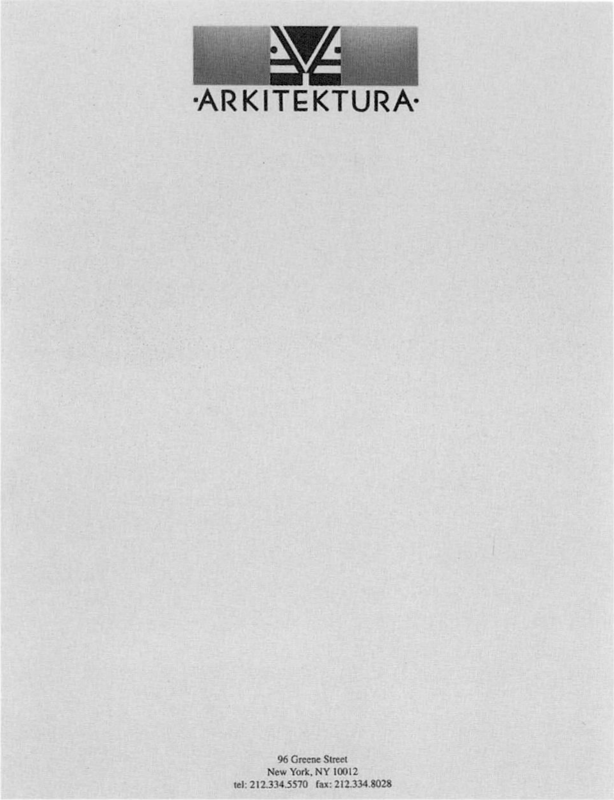

·ARKITEKTURA·

96 Greene Street
New York, NY 10012
tel: 212.334.5570 fax: 212.334.8028

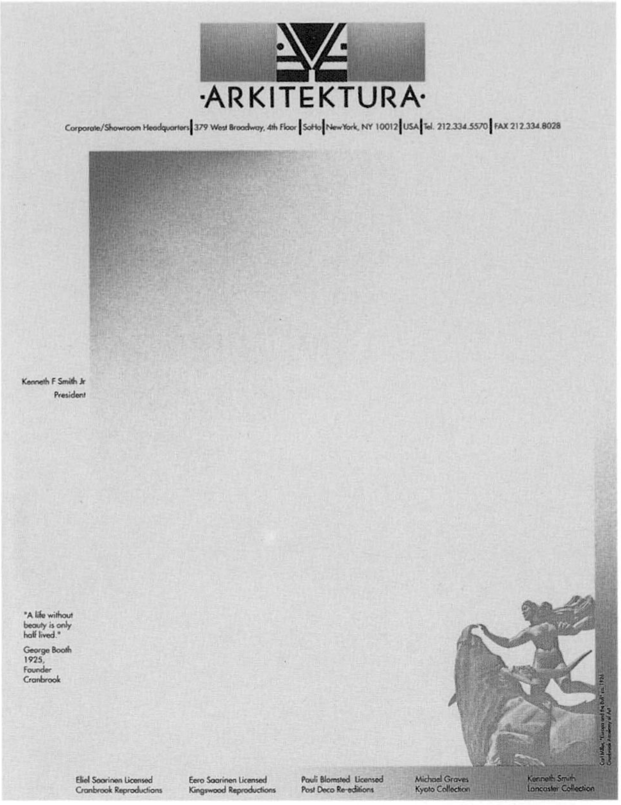

·ARKITEKTURA·

Corporate/Showroom Headquarters | 379 West Broadway, 4th Floor | SoHo | NewYork, NY 10012 | USA | Tel. 212.334.5570 | FAX 212.334.8028

Kenneth F Smith Jr
President

"A life without beauty is only half lived."
George Booth
1925,
Founder
Cranbrook

Eliel Saarinen Licensed Cranbrook Reproductions
Eero Saarinen Licensed Kingswood Reproductions
Pauli Blomsted Licensed Post Deco Re-editions
Michael Graves Kyoto Collection
Kenneth Smith Lancaster Collection

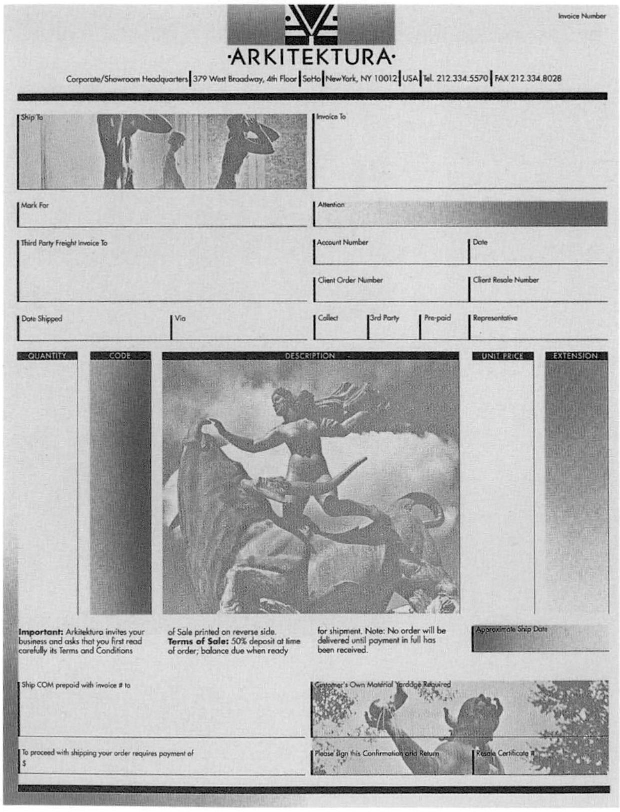

Invoice Number

·ARKITEKTURA·

Corporate/Showroom Headquarters | 379 West Broadway, 4th Floor | SoHo | NewYork, NY 10012 | USA | Tel. 212.334.5570 | FAX 212.334.8028

Ship To
Invoice To
Mark For
Attention
Third Party Freight Invoice To
Account Number
Date
Client Order Number
Client Resale Number
Date Shipped
Via
Collect
3rd Party
Pre-paid
Representative

QUANTITY	CODE	DESCRIPTION	UNIT PRICE	EXTENSION

Important: Arkitektura invites your business and asks that you first read carefully its Terms and Conditions of Sale printed on reverse side. **Terms of Sale:** 50% deposit at time of order; balance due when ready for shipment. Note: No order will be delivered until payment in full has been received.

Approximate Ship Date
Ship COM prepaid with invoice # to
Customer's Own Material Yardage Required
To proceed with shipping your order requires payment of
$
Please Sign this Confirmation and Return
Resale Certificate #

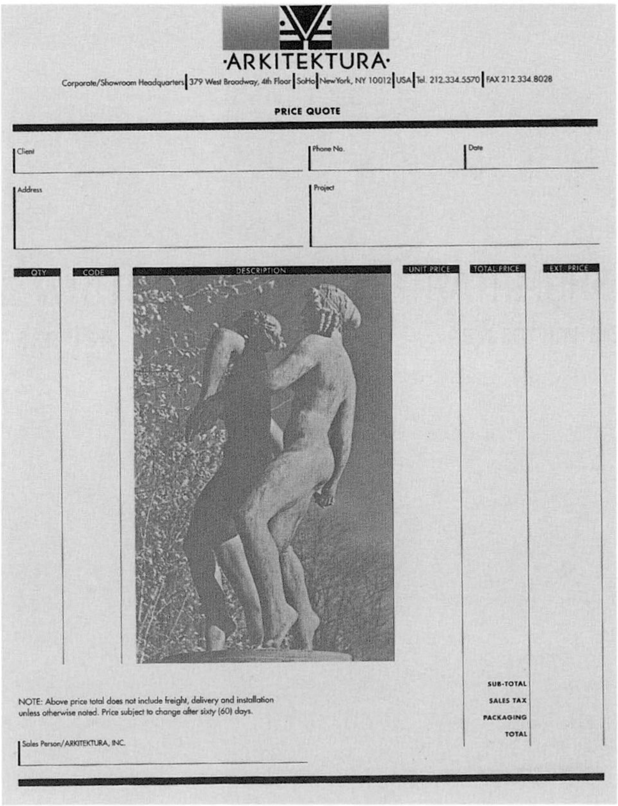

·ARKITEKTURA·

Corporate/Showroom Headquarters | 379 West Broadway, 4th Floor | SoHo | NewYork, NY 10012 | USA | Tel. 212.334.5570 | FAX 212.334.8028

PRICE QUOTE

Client
Phone No.
Date
Address
Project

QTY	CODE	DESCRIPTION	UNIT PRICE	TOTAL PRICE	EXT. PRICE

SUB-TOTAL
SALES TAX
PACKAGING
TOTAL

NOTE: Above price total does not include freight, delivery and installation unless otherwise noted. Price subject to change after sixty (60) days.

Sales Person/ARKITEKTURA, INC.

ARKITEKTURA

COUNTRY OF ORIGIN: America

DESIGNER: Kenneth F. Smith Jnr

DATE: 1994

TYPE OF IDENTITY IMPLEMENTATION: Complete identity

TARGET AUDIENCE: General public

CLIENT'S BRIEF: To create a striking and bold logo in keeping with the merchandise on sale. To capture the spirit of imagination

DESIGN RATIONALE: An art deco typeface was chosen and a similar motif designed. Both are carried on all aspects of packaging and correspondence paper. The imposed images have been dropped on headed paper and compliment slips to simplify the house style and attract greater attention to the logo itself

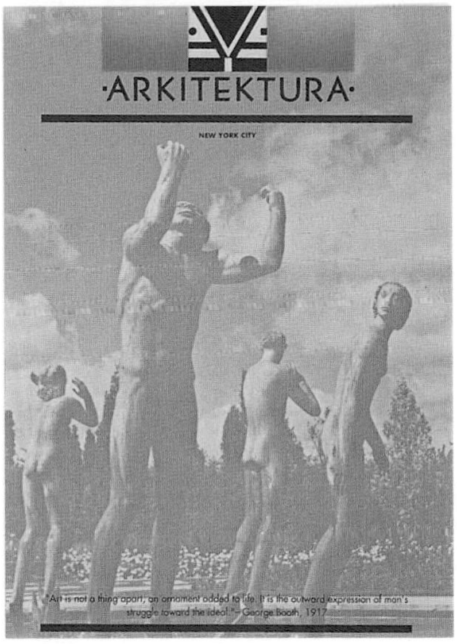

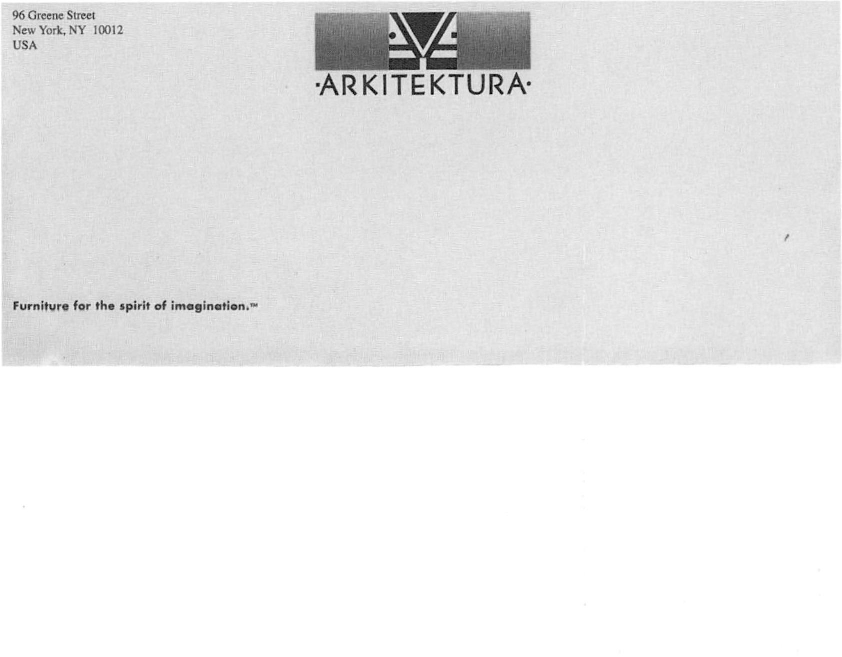

FOOD & BEVERAGES

2

GALL & GALL
BITTERS
BESSEN
Voor de betere Franse wijnen moet u in Zuid-Amerika zijn (of bij ons).
GALL & GALL
MARCUS JAMES

wijn-
kelder

Gall & Gall

COUNTRY OF ORIGIN: The Netherlands

DESIGNER: 20/20 Design & Strategy Consultants, London, England

DATE: 1993

TYPE OF IDENTITY IMPLEMENTATION: Complete store identity

TARGET AUDIENCE: The Dutch off-licence shopper, the wine drinker

CLIENT'S BRIEF: To consolidate the chain of outlets, which had grown largely by acquisition under one new concept. To untap the potential of the fastest growing and most profitable of the market – wine sales

DESIGN RATIONALE: A new approach to merchandise groupings, presentation and attitudes to service was developed. The ambience of the whole store was readdressed, introducing wine, beer and liquor signals to their best effect. The trading identity was revisited with changes to colour and form whilst retaining the basic typeface. The combination of this and a new illustration style provided Gall & Gall with a powerful and flexible visual theme for customer communications

Harnett's

COUNTRY OF ORIGIN: America

DESIGNER: Mary Lewis, Melanie Lowe, Michele Phelan, Clifford Selbert/Clifford Selbert Design Collaborative, Cambridge, Massachusetts, USA

DATE: 1993 September

TYPE OF IDENTITY IMPLEMENTATION: Complete store identity

TARGET AUDIENCE: General public

CLIENT'S BRIEF: To design an identity for an alternative natural pharmacy that was warm, simple and inviting. Due to the wide variety of products in the stores a quiet and peaceful atmosphere was needed

DESIGN RATIONALE: The typography of the logo mimics the old apothecary style. Colours are natural with a soft graduation. In keeping with the 'all natural' philosophy, the design is very simple

PHOTOGRAPHER: Anton Grassl

PRINTER: Design Communications, USA

HARNETT'S

HARNETT'S

HARNETT'S
HARNETT'S
BONESET
$18.55 LB

Carluccio's

COUNTRY OF ORIGIN: United Kingdom

DESIGNER: Jonathan Stewart

DATE: 1991 October

TYPE OF IDENTITY IMPLEMENTATION: Bags, stationery, packaging, fascia, internal signage

TARGET AUDIENCE: General public, Italian food lovers

CLIENT'S BRIEF: To create classic Italian quality food, to be contemporary but not avant-garde. The branding had to be suitable for an international umbrella brand in the future

DESIGN RATIONALE: Each product has an unique concept even though the house style is similar. As products are shelved together the brands are strongly designed but remain interesting and reflect the contents

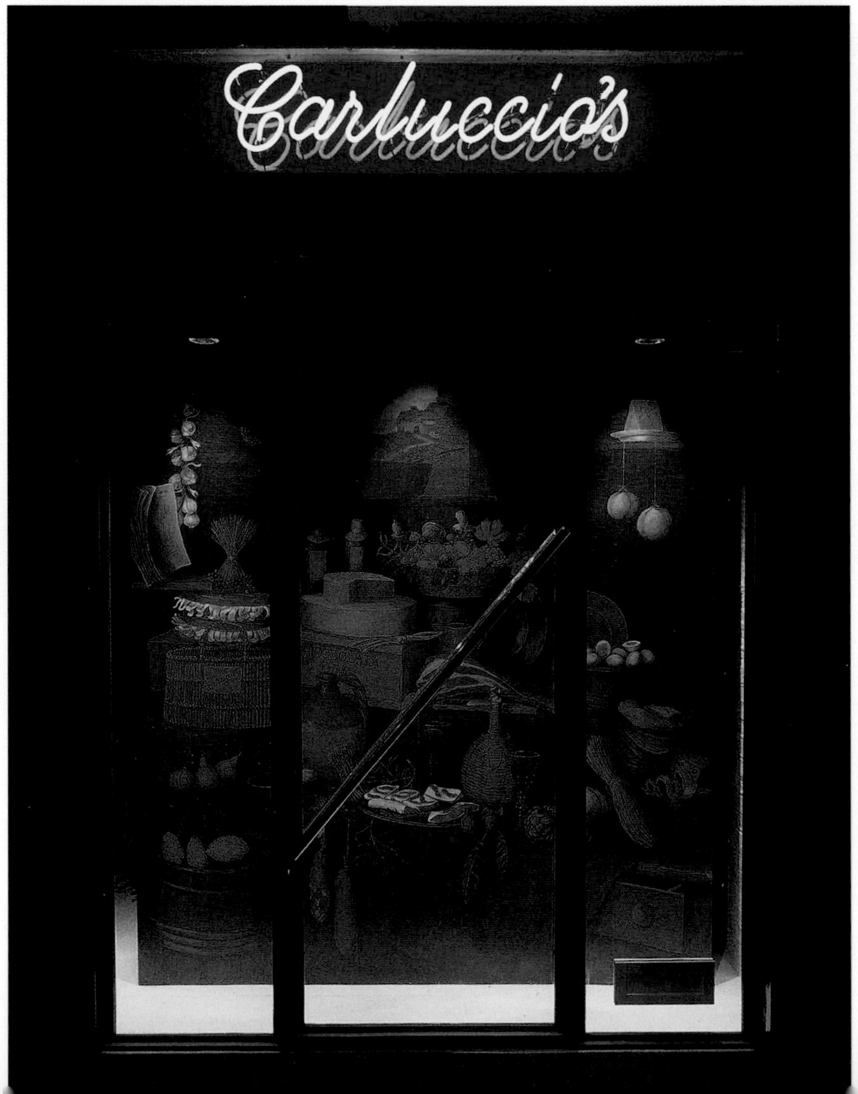

Carluccio's
Carluccio's

Alldays

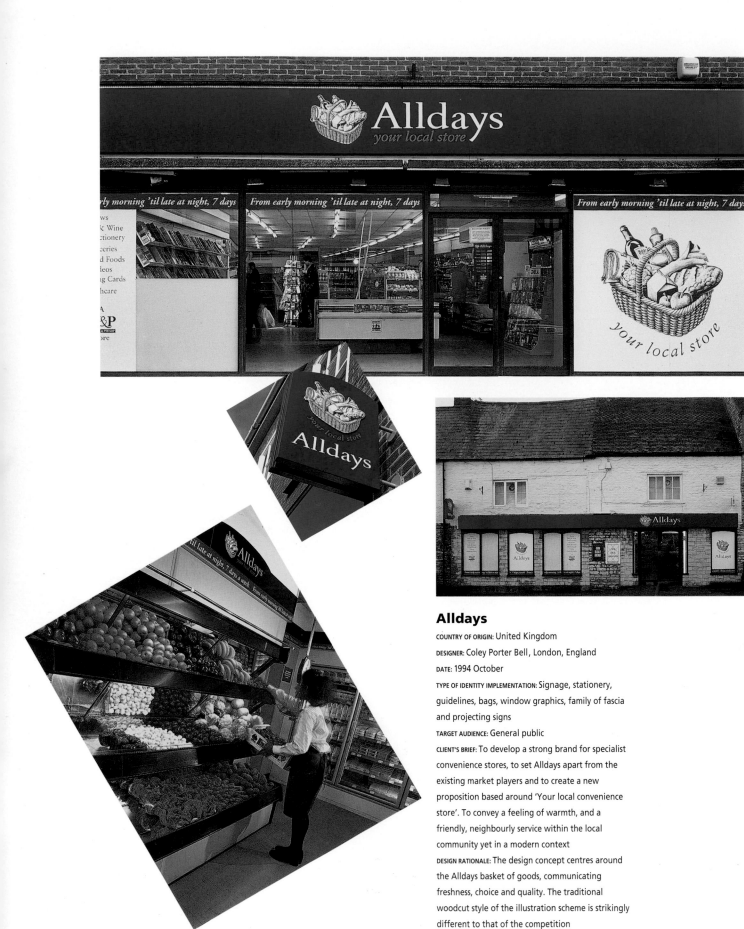

COUNTRY OF ORIGIN: United Kingdom

DESIGNER: Coley Porter Bell, London, England

DATE: 1994 October

TYPE OF IDENTITY IMPLEMENTATION: Signage, stationery, guidelines, bags, window graphics, family of fascia and projecting signs

TARGET AUDIENCE: General public

CLIENT'S BRIEF: To develop a strong brand for specialist convenience stores, to set Alldays apart from the existing market players and to create a new proposition based around 'Your local convenience store'. To convey a feeling of warmth, and a friendly, neighbourly service within the local community yet in a modern context

DESIGN RATIONALE: The design concept centres around the Alldays basket of goods, communicating freshness, choice and quality. The traditional woodcut style of the illustration scheme is strikingly different to that of the competition

Maison Blanc

COUNTRY OF ORIGIN: United Kingdom

DESIGNER: Rod Petrie, Graham Shearsby/Design Bridge, London, England

DATE: 1991 Flagship store – 1993 other branches

TYPE OF IDENTITY IMPLEMENTATION: Bags, stationery, signage, product packaging

TARGET AUDIENCE: Connoisseurs of French pâtisseries

CLIENT'S BRIEF: To create a new identity which could be subsequently reapplied to additional stores

DESIGN RATIONALE: The inspiration behind the rather quirky logo came from the attractive 'twirly' bits which are so prevalent in French pâtisserie. We retained the pink theme from the previous incarnation but used it in a more decorative and stylish way. The carrier bag was designed to act as a vibrant poster for the shop

FOOD
GIANT

AMAZIN'
SAVIN'S
20
21

3
21
22

AMAZIN'
SAVIN'S

Food Giant

COUNTRY OF ORIGIN: United Kingdom

DESIGNER: David S. Mackay/Crabtree Hall, London, England and Plan Créatif, Paris, France

DATE: 1991

TYPE OF IDENTITY IMPLEMENTATION: Complete store identity

TARGET AUDIENCE: Cost-conscious family shoppers

CLIENT'S BRIEF: To provide a colourful and distinctive design concept which could be implemented rapidly and at low cost to act as an antidote to the universally dull and understated competitive environment

DESIGN RATIONALE: The design was conceived as a highly colourful humorous response to the conventional 'non-design' discount market. Given the low client expenditure the solution was essentially graphic and cosmetic, a 'comic book' response in an otherwise dull market sector

Icky, Sticky & Goo
ISG

ISG
Gifts & Goodies
ISG
Unlimited

Icy, Sticky & Goo

COUNTRY OF ORIGIN: America

DESIGNER: James Keane/Kibu Obata & Co, St. Louis, Missouri, USA and Idie McGinty, Tim McGinty, Jane McNeely, Sylvia Teng/AIA, USA

DATE: 1994 Summer

TYPE OF IDENTITY IMPLEMENTATION: Prototype candy store including overall concept, name, identity, store design, visual merchandising, signage and graphics

TARGET AUDIENCE: General public

CLIENT'S BRIEF: To create this fictitious candy corporation to promote Icy, Sticky & Goo

DESIGN RATIONALE: Three animated characters were designed, Kar Mel Icky, Sterling Sticky & Miss Divinity Goo who serve as the company's founders. The prototype store has 'corporate touches' throughout including fixtures that look like roll-top desks, chandeliers and the company logo inlaid into the floor at the entrance. Bright colours and playful images create a whimsical candy corporation that elicits both a smile from the customer and an instant feeling of welcome

PHOTOGRAPHER: Ed Massery

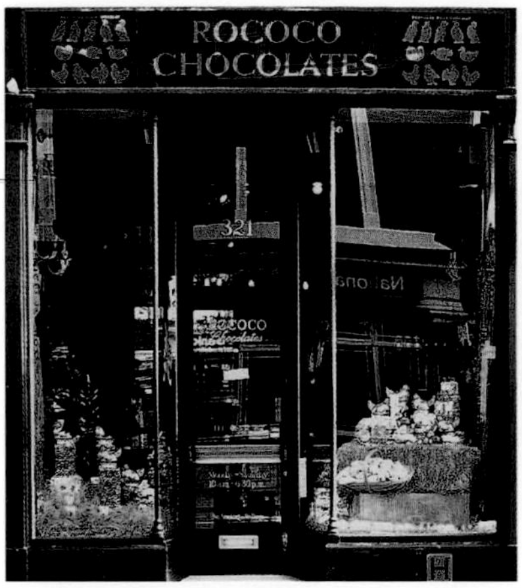

Rococo Chocolates

COUNTRY OF ORIGIN: United Kingdom

DESIGNER: Chantal Coady/Rococo Chocolates, London, England

DATE: 1982 March

TYPE OF IDENTITY IMPLEMENTATION: Complete store identity

TARGET AUDIENCE: General public

CLIENT'S BRIEF: To create a memorable, easily identifiable branding by using an old chocolate mould catalogue and labels

DESIGN RATIONALE: Pages from an old catalogue were used to create a random repeat design, suitable for wrapping boxes and bars. The colour is used for the fascia and shop fittings. Labels appear to be hand written using a special 'Rococo' alphabet

CATALOGUE: 1906 L'Etang Fils-Paris

FRENCH ALPHABET: Didier de Cottignies

PHOTOGRAPHER: Paul Crossman for ES Magazine and Neil Pinnock

SIGNMAKER: John Farnham

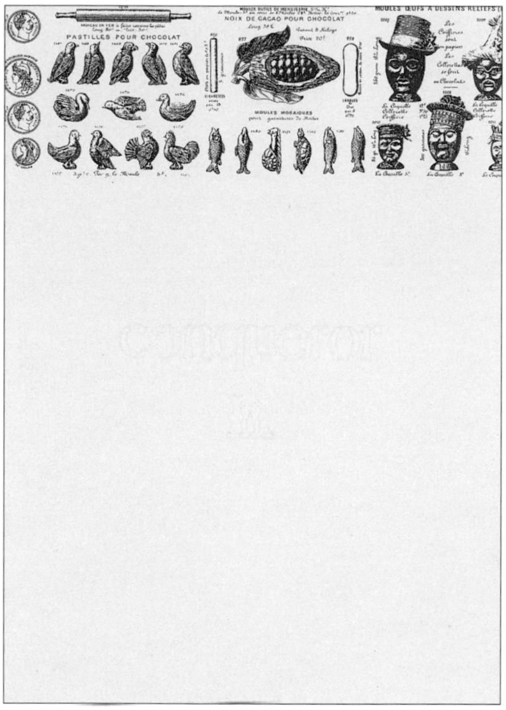
PASTILLES POUR CHOCOLAT
NOIX DE CACAO POUR CHOCOLAT
MOULES MOSAIQUES

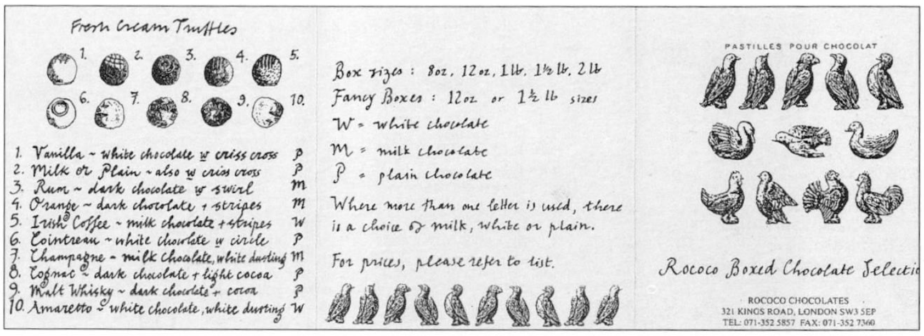
From Cream Truffles
1. Vanilla ~ white chocolate w criss cross P
2. Milk or Plain ~ also w criss cross P
3. Rum ~ dark chocolate w swirl M
4. Orange ~ dark chocolate + stripes M
5. Irish Coffee ~ milk chocolate + stripes W
6. Cointreau ~ white chocolate w circle P
7. Champagne ~ milk chocolate, white dusting M
8. Cognac ~ dark chocolate + light cocoa P
9. Malt Whisky ~ dark chocolate + cocoa P
10. Amaretto ~ white chocolate, white dusting W
Box sizes : 8oz, 12oz, 1lb, 1½lb, 2lb
Fancy Boxes : 12oz or 1½ lb sizes
W = white chocolate
M = milk chocolate
P = plain chocolate
Where more than one letter is used, there is a choice of milk, white or plain.
For prices, please refer to list.
PASTILLES POUR CHOCOLAT
Rococo Boxed Chocolate Selection
ROCOCO CHOCOLATES
321 KINGS ROAD, LONDON SW3 5EP
TEL: 071-352 5857 FAX: 071-352 7360

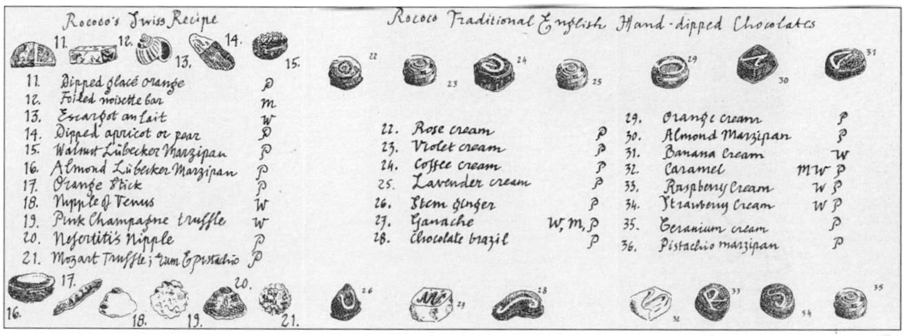
Rococo's Swiss Recipe
11. Dipped glacé orange P
12. Foiled noisette bar M
13. Escargot au lait W
14. Dipped apricot or pear P
15. Walnut Lübecker Marzipan P
16. Almond Lübecker Marzipan P
17. Orange Stick P
18. Nipple of Venus W
19. Pink Champagne truffle W
20. Nefertiti's Nipple P
21. Mozart Truffle; rum & pistachio P
Rococo Traditional English Hand-dipped Chocolates
22. Rose cream P
23. Violet cream P
24. Coffee cream P
25. Lavender cream P
26. Stem ginger P
27. Ganache W, M, P
28. Chocolate brazil P
29. Orange cream P
30. Almond Marzipan P
31. Banana Cream W
32. Caramel M W P
33. Raspberry Cream W P
34. Strawberry Cream W P
35. Geranium cream P
36. Pistachio marzipan P

PASTILLES POUR CHOCOLAT
321 KING'S ROAD
TEL: 071-352 5857
ROCOCO CHOCOLATES

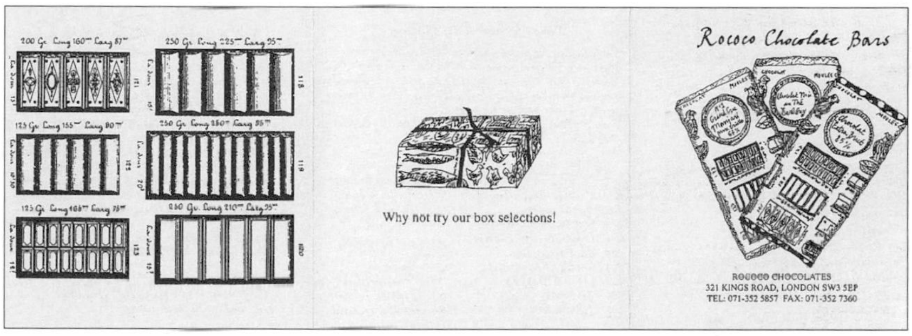
Why not try our box selections!
Rococo Chocolate Bars
ROCOCO CHOCOLATES
321 KINGS ROAD, LONDON SW3 5EP
TEL: 071-352 5857 FAX: 071-352 7360

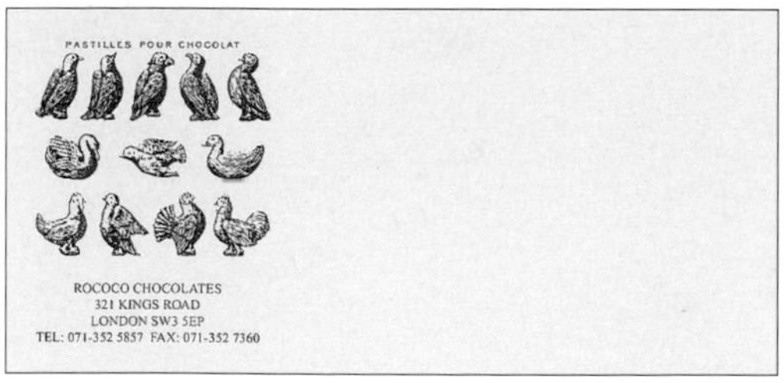
PASTILLES POUR CHOCOLAT
ROCOCO CHOCOLATES
321 KINGS ROAD
LONDON SW3 5EP
TEL: 071-352 5857 FAX: 071-352 7360

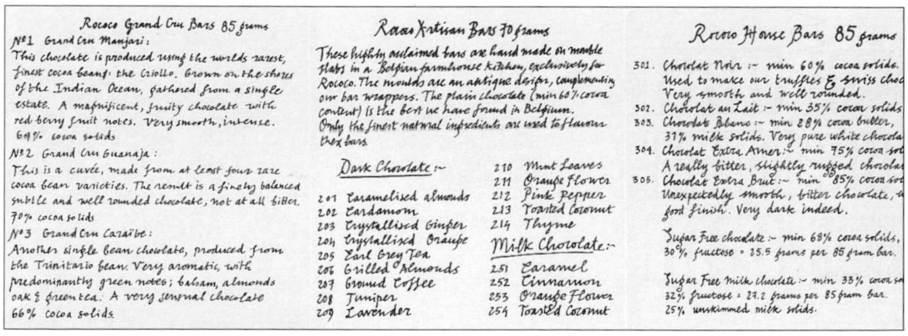
Rococo Grand Cru Bars 85 grams
Nº1 Grand Cru Manjari:
This chocolate is produced using the worlds rarest, finest cocoa beans: the Criollo. Grown on the shores of the Indian Ocean, gathered from a single estate. A magnificent, fruity chocolate with red berry fruit notes. Very smooth, intense. 64% cocoa solids
Nº2 Grand Cru Guanaja:
This is a cuvée, made from at least four rare cocoa bean varieties. The result is a finely balanced subtle and well rounded chocolate, not at all bitter. 70% cocoa solids
Nº3 Grand Cru Caraïbe:
Another single bean chocolate, produced from the Trinitario bean. Very aromatic, with predominantly green notes; balsam, almonds oak & green tea. A very sensual chocolate 66% cocoa solids.
Rococo Artisan Bars 70 grams
These highly acclaimed bars are hand made on marble slabs in a Belgian farmhouse kitchen, exclusively for Rococo. The moulds are an antique design, complementing our bar wrappers. The plain chocolate (min 60% cocoa content) is the best we have found in Belgium. Only the finest natural ingredients are used to flavour these bars.
Dark Chocolate:~
201 Caramelised almonds
202 Cardamom
203 Crystallised Ginger
204 Crystallised Orange
205 Earl Grey Tea
206 Grilled Almonds
207 Ground Coffee
208 Juniper
209 Lavender
210 Mint Leaves
211 Orange Flower
212 Pink Pepper
213 Toasted Coconut
214 Thyme
Milk Chocolate:~
251 Caramel
252 Cinnamon
253 Orange Flower
254 Toasted Coconut
Rococo House Bars 85 grams
301. Chocolat Noir :~ min 60% cocoa solids. Used to make our truffles & swiss choc… Very smooth and well rounded.
302. Chocolat au Lait :~ min 35% cocoa solids
303. Chocolat Blanc :~ min 28% cocoa butter, 31% milk solids. Very pure white chocola…
304. Chocolat Extra Amer :~ min 75% cocoa so… A really bitter, slightly rugged chocola…
305. Chocolat Extra Brut :~ min 85% cocoa so… Unexpectedly smooth, bitter chocolate, … good finish. Very dark indeed.
Sugar Free chocolate :~ min 68% cocoa solids, 30% fructose = 25.5 grams per 85 gram bar.
Sugar Free milk chocolate :~ min 33% cocoa so… 32% fructose = 27.2 grams per 85 gram bar. 25% unskimmed milk solids.

PASTILLES POUR CHOCOLAT
ROCOCO CHOCOLATES
321 Kings Road
London SW3 5EP
Tel: 071-352 5857

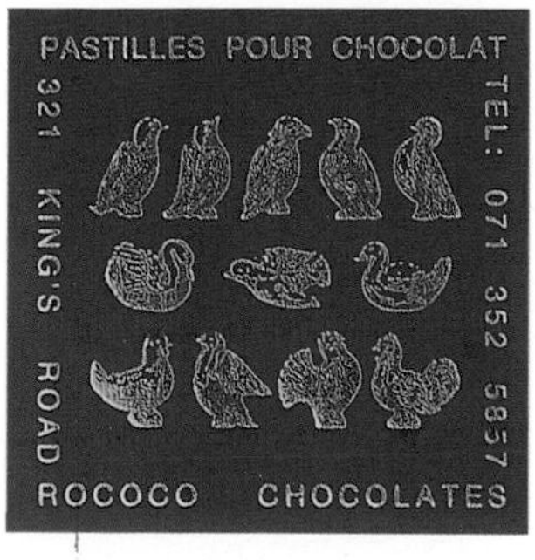
PASTILLES POUR CHOCOLAT
321 KING'S ROAD
TEL: 071 352 5857
ROCOCO CHOCOLATES

Mr Chips

COUNTRY OF ORIGIN: America

DESIGNER: Seymour Chwast/The Pushpin Group, New York, USA

DATE: 1994 Summer

TYPE OF IDENTITY IMPLEMENTATION: Stationery and ice-cream cups and T-shirts

TARGET AUDIENCE: General public

CLIENT'S BRIEF: To create a brand name for this new ice-cream outlet

DESIGN RATIONALE: Clean and simple, eye-catching graphics were used to create a playful identity that would appeal to both children and adults. A 'cute' character, Mr Chips, was created to develop the image further

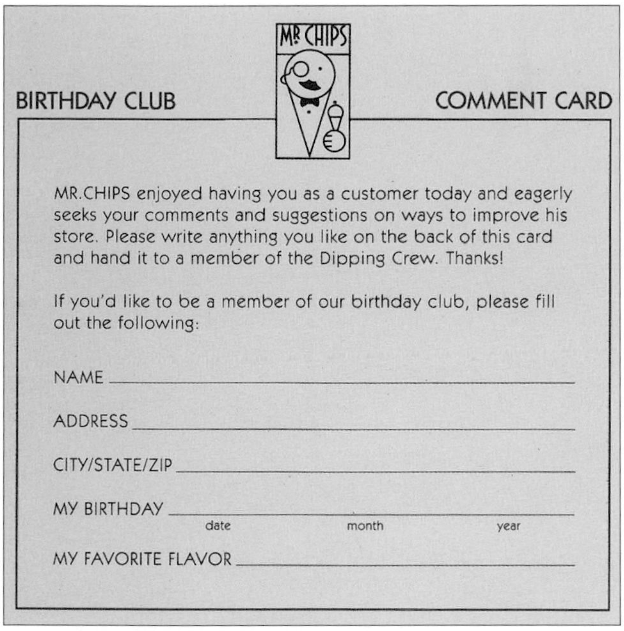

BIRTHDAY CLUB   MR. CHIPS   COMMENT CARD

MR.CHIPS enjoyed having you as a customer today and eagerly seeks your comments and suggestions on ways to improve his store. Please write anything you like on the back of this card and hand it to a member of the Dipping Crew. Thanks!

If you'd like to be a member of our birthday club, please fill out the following:

NAME ____________________

ADDRESS ____________________

CITY/STATE/ZIP ____________________

MY BIRTHDAY ____________________
date   month   year

MY FAVORITE FLAVOR ____________________

MR. CHIPS
CHIP FISHER
PRESIDENT
27 EAST 92 STREET • NEW YORK, NY 10128 • (212) 831 5555

Fuller's Wine Merchants

COUNTRY OF ORIGIN: United Kingdom

DESIGNER: Design House, London, England

DATE: 1990

TYPE OF IDENTITY IMPLEMENTATION: Complete identity

TARGET AUDIENCE: All wine lovers

CLIENT'S BRIEF: To take advantage of the growth in popularity of wine by repositioning the brand as a quality wine merchants whilst creating a welcoming and accessible atmosphere to the average customer

DESIGN RATIONALE: The design aims to communicate accessible quality by providing plenty of information, often with a quirky, humorous touch. A wide variety of formal and informal merchandising techniques provide interest, while encouraging hands-on experience of the product by customers. The distinct identity developed for the wine merchants shops nevertheless retains the distinguishing features of the Fuller's brand

WINE MERCHA
OPEN
BURGUNDY
AUTUMN
3 BOTTLES
FOR
£6.99
ANY
COMBINATION
FAMOUS
GROUSE
£10.79
HIGH
&
DRY
£8.45
£5.55
£5.99

GRIFFIN BREWERY
FULLER'S
CHISWICK

SPORT & LEISURE

3

Going Places

COUNTRY OF ORIGIN: United Kingdom

DESIGNER: Coley Porter Bell, London, England

DATE: 1993 December

TYPE OF IDENTITY IMPLEMENTATION: Retail signage, fascias, stationery, promotional items, bags, ticketing, design guidelines

TARGET AUDIENCE: Mass market, families, holiday buyers

CLIENT'S BRIEF: To create a new brand for a high street travel agency, encompassing two newly acquired travel chains. To create a new name to prompt the response 'holidays for everyone'. To successfully integrate the new agency into the Airtours culture

DESIGN RATIONALE: A unique presence was created. Working within the Airtours' corporate palette of blue, red and green, we added a bright yellow to bring an element of fun, and develop a visual identity which uses an abstract representation of the sun, sea and palm tree to evoke the 'quintessential' holiday

Going Places

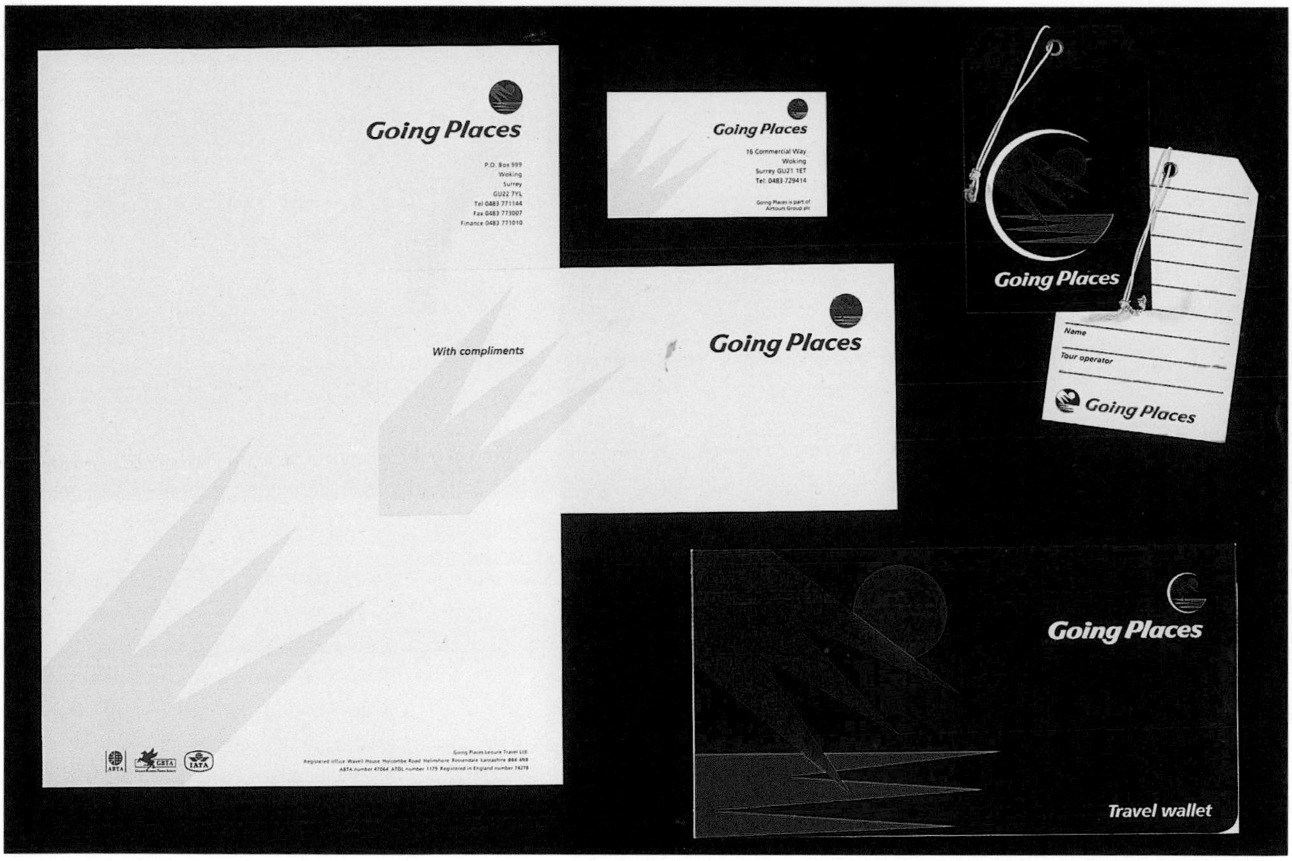
Going Places
P.O. Box 999
Woking
Surrey
GU22 7YL
Tel 0483 771144
Fax 0483 773007
Finance 0483 771010
Going Places
16 Commercial Way
Woking
Surrey GU21 1ET
Tel: 0483 729414
With compliments
Going Places
Going Places
Name
Tour operator
Going Places
Going Places
Travel wallet

PSYC

COUNTRY OF ORIGIN: United Kingdom
DESIGNER: Chris Dewar Dixon, Gregor Jackson/Four IV, London, England
DATE: 1992 September
TYPE OF IDENTITY IMPLEMENTATION: Swing ticket, bag, stationery, clothing brand, fascia
TARGET AUDIENCE: Fitness enthusiasts
CLIENT'S BRIEF: To capitalise on the fitness and dance market through the creation of a sophisticated dancewear and aerobic fitness/dance studio
DESIGN RATIONALE: The PSYC name is an abbreviation of physical. Handrawn type reflected the grace and movement associated with dance. The site's relatively small frontage and imposing entrance was formed with a full height glass display window to one side with a textured curved wall and a suspended curved stainless steel gate opposite. Soft neutral colours are used throughout; dove grey ceramic floor tiles, white walls and pale maple timber doors throughout created a fresh serene atmosphere which allowed the quality, style, and colours of the clothing to take precedence. Simple white partition walls formed the divisions between each merchandise bay and allowed a progressive revealing of the range of clothing as the customer moves through the space. Each bay was organised to allow both forward and side hanging, broken by only two glass shelves per bay to take folded items

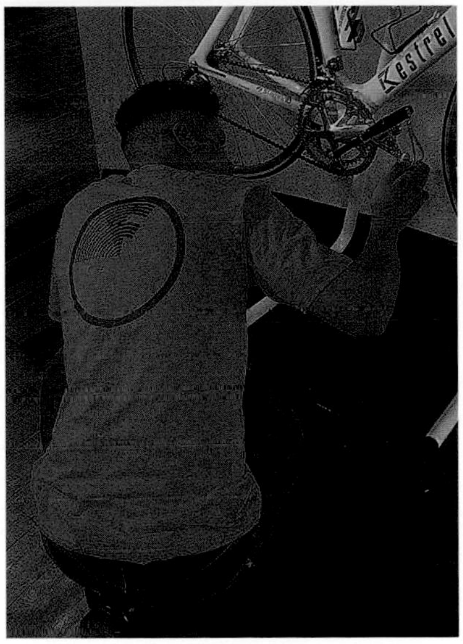

Freewheel

COUNTRY OF ORIGIN: United Kingdom

DESIGNER: Philip Carter, Graham Simpson/CWSH Designers, London, England

DATE: 1989

TYPE OF IDENTITY IMPLEMENTATION: Bags, graphic banners, swing tickets, catalogue, internal signage, interior design, shop fascia, display systems

TARGET AUDIENCE: Both serious and fun cyclists, all ages

CLIENT'S BRIEF: Freewheel cycles and accessories had previously been marketed solely by mail order catalogue. CWSH were invited to create a new identity and design system for an entire range of franchise stores

DESIGN RATIONALE: Cycling had moved on from being seen as an old fashioned mode of transport, to a highly desirable sporting activity. The bold 'F' identity, combined with the interior design featuring a central hub cash desk and bright graphic banners dividing the space, were created to reflect this change

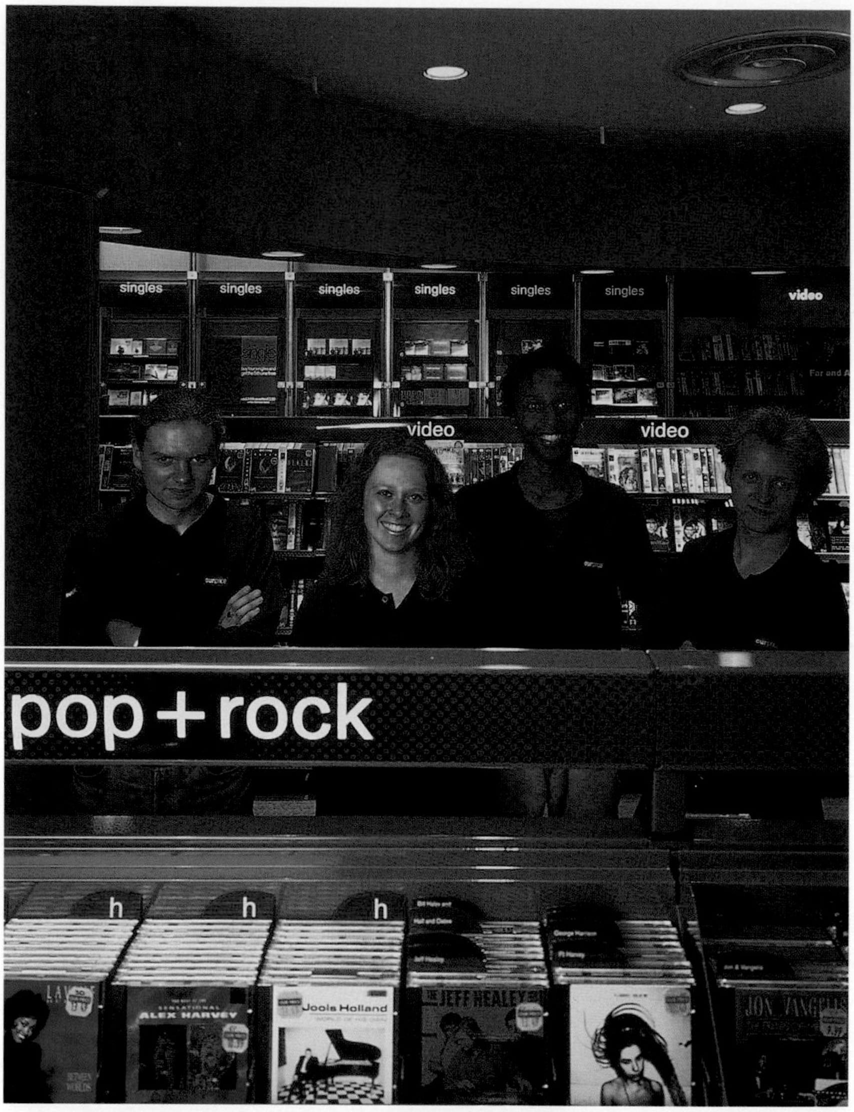

Our Price Ltd

COUNTRY OF ORIGIN: United Kingdom

DESIGNER: Nicholas Thirkell/CDT Design Ltd, London, England

DATE: 1993 March

TYPE OF IDENTITY IMPLEMENTATION: All aspects: fascia, internal signage, point-of-sale guidelines, logo and logotype, stationery, corporate manual, carrier bags, gift vouchers, staff uniforms

TARGET AUDIENCE: Music buyers

CLIENT'S BRIEF: Our Price were well known in the market place, yet research showed that stores were regarded as 'dull, boring and drab'. This prompted a brand repositioning initiative providing new products to customers which were easy to find and competitively priced and sold within an enticing environment

DESIGN RATIONALE: The new logo was based on a compact disk which was separated from the logotype. The red and white were retained because of their strength and Our Price familiarity. Typography was refined to present a clean and contemporary feel. Colour zones were devised to define product areas, Chart Albums were clearly numbered, counters lowered and the new advertising strategy all contributed to a shopping environment that was less confusing than before

ADDITIONAL CREDITS: Iain Crockart, Neil Walker/CDT Design

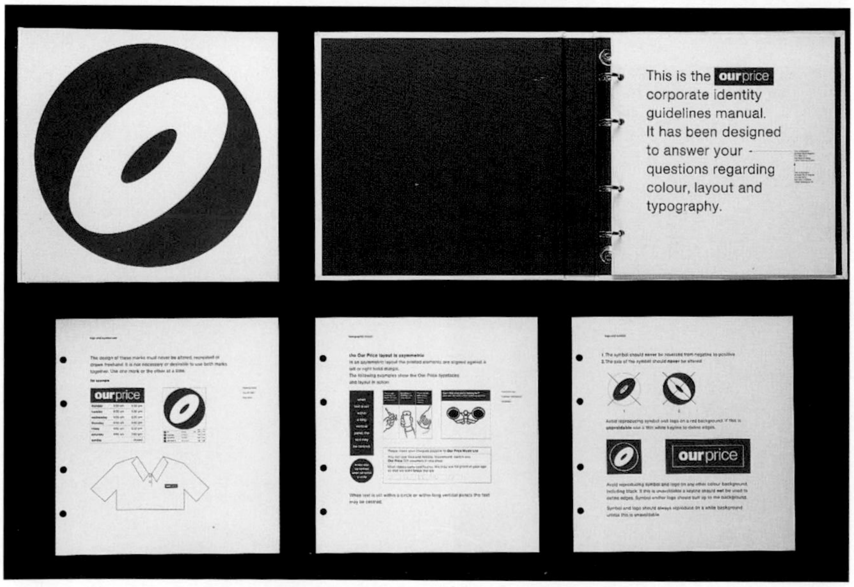

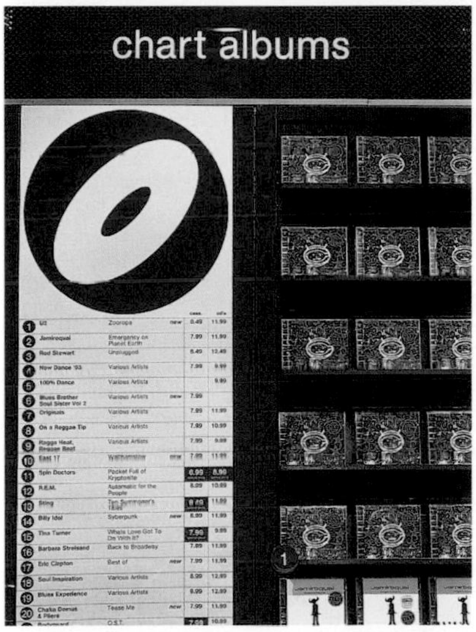
chart albums

compact discs
Like what you're hearing?
Just ask us for details at the counter.
Looking for a particular title?
Just ask, we'll order it for you at no extra charge.
folk
jazz
RIO BY NIGHT

cd sampler

our top 10 games
games
our top 10 games

singles
no risk disc
you'll love our new cds

Virgin Megastore, Oxford Street

COUNTRY OF ORIGIN: United Kingdom

DESIGNER: 20/20 Design & Strategy Consultants, London, England

DATE: 1995 June

TYPE OF IDENTITY IMPLEMENTATION: Environment, in-store communications

TARGET AUDIENCE: 16–35 year old music, video and games shoppers

CLIENT'S BRIEF: To create a land mark and flagship store for the Virgin brand and Megastore chain

DESIGN RATIONALE: Harnessing the innovations of their 1990 Megastore concept, 20/20 set out to ensure that the Oxford Street Megastore at 70,000 square feet, the world's biggest entertainment outlet was the ultimate adrenalin pumping retailing experience. Unique and dramatic features were introduced befitting the stores landmark status and the 'personalities' of each of the departments were developed. Together with the Design Clinic, 20/20 introduced a graphic communications programme to allow customers to shop in large spaces with consumate ease. The central design feature is the 70ft atrium and information tower which bisects the entire fourth floor trading space providing both drama and a means to encourage vertical circulation

PHOTOGRAPHY: Jon O'Brien

classical
THE MEGASTORE

THE MEGASTORE

PAY HERE

First Floor
Classical. Video
Specialist Music
Jazz
Country
Films & Shows
Listen
Listen

HMV, Leeds

COUNTRY OF ORIGIN: United Kingdom
DESIGNER: Martyn Bullock, Richard Greenleaf/Red Jacket, London, England
DATE: 1994 October
TYPE OF IDENTITY IMPLEMENTATION: Environmental and internal signage
TARGET AUDIENCE: A broad-based record buying public
CLIENT'S BRIEF: To create a store concept that is exciting and unique, purchase compelling whilst being sympathetic to the differing attitudes of music consumers
DESIGN RATIONALE: Lighting, bold graphics and strong colour create an exciting and unforgettable experience akin to attending a rock concert

Speedo Authentic Fitness

COUNTRY OF ORIGIN: America

DESIGNER: Harvey Bernstein/Berstein Design Associates, New York, USA

DATE: 1992

TYPE OF IDENTITY IMPLEMENTATION: Complete store design including stationery, bags, internal signage

TARGET AUDIENCE: Mass market

CLIENT'S BRIEF: To create a store prototype concept and fixture programme that is exciting, product specific and that can be easily repeated across America in three weeks

DESIGN RATIONALE: Utilising the imagery of the swimming pool and gym, the stores (60 completed) features an upside-down swimming pool complete with moving water (an illusion) on the ceiling and the fixtures emphasise the swim/gym focus

AUTHENTIC FITNESS
FITNESS BASICS
BAR BELL

Cobra

COUNTRY OF ORIGIN: United Kingdom
DESIGNER: Mike Jewitt/Metropolis 88 Design Group, London, England
DATE: 1995 February
TYPE OF IDENTITY IMPLEMENTATION: Fascia, merchandising system, bags, point-of-sale, internal signage, corporate communications
TARGET AUDIENCE: Athletic market, 15–25 year olds
CLIENT'S BRIEF: To develop an identity and corporate colour palette which reflected the excitement of sport. The identity had to expand within the store and give design direction to a wide variety of elements from fascia, store directory, till unit to product descriptor cards
DESIGN RATIONALE: Sports retailers suffer from visual domination by the brands stockers, competitive outlets can become clones, ostensibly the same. Design, therefore concentrated on developing strong Cobra branding communicated through colour, materials, shapes and wall mark features such as the bag, fascia and till units

cobra

CATERPILLAR
CHEVIGNON
NORTHERN EXTREME
ELLESSE
TIMBERLAND
FRONTIER APPAREL
AMERICAN LICENSED CLOTHING
ACCESSORIES
NO FEAR
cobra
FIRST
CLOTHING
REEBOK
NIKE
ADIDAS
MENS SPORTSWEAR
WOMENS FITNESS AND LEISURE
SOCCER TRAINING
FOOTWEAR
BASKETBALL
X-TRAINING
RUNNING
CLASSICS
YOUTHS
FOOTBALL
CUSTOMER SERVICES

Coral

COUNTRY OF ORIGIN: United Kingdom

DESIGNER: Gordon Bremner/Light & Coley Ltd, London, England

DATE: 1992 and 1995 revised through deregulation

TYPE OF IDENTITY IMPLEMENTATION: Complete identity

TARGET AUDIENCE: Existing betting shop customers and potential new customers

CLIENT'S BRIEF: To move the image and operating methods of Coral away from that of a traditional bookmaker and move towards a more leisure oriented, high traffic flow, multisized retail environment. To provide a perception amongst target consumers of an added value betting experience

DESIGN RATIONALE: Through the use of a bold colours, clean shapes and an eye-catching logo a fresh and exciting approach gives the organisation a new and contemporary feel

CORAL
OPEN
THIS
SUNDAY
FULL SUNDAY
RACING CALENDAR
AVAILABLE HERE
IN ANY EVENT, CORAL IT.
CORAL
LITTLE OODS
VERNONS
POOLS COUPONS
AND INFORMATION
AVAILABLE HERE
IN ANY EVENT, CORAL IT.
CORAL

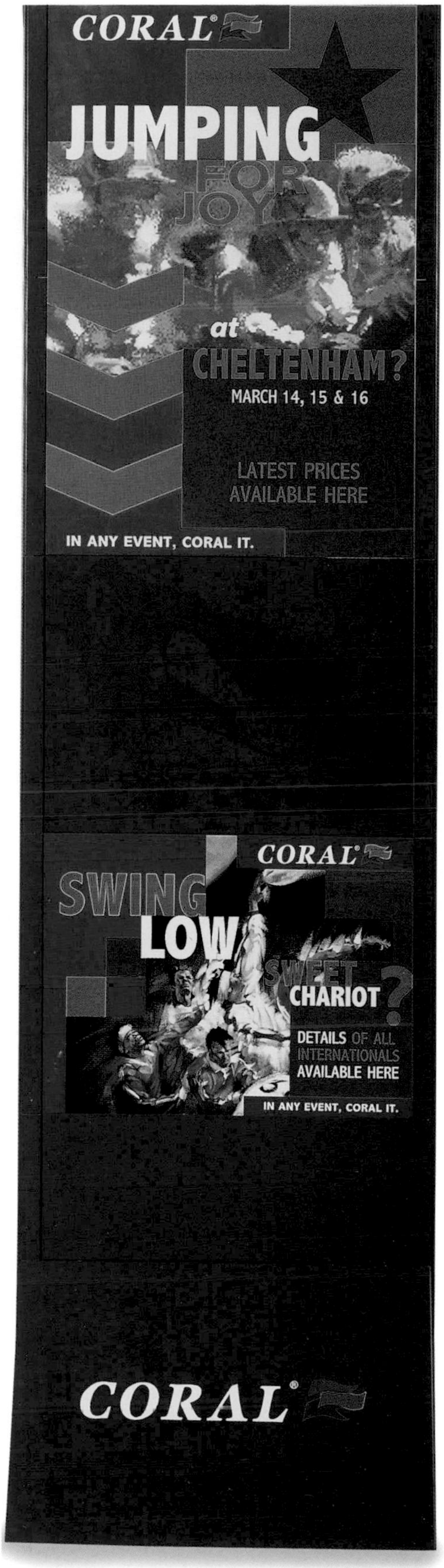
CORAL
JUMPING
FOR
JOY
at
CHELTENHAM?
MARCH 14, 15 & 16
LATEST PRICES
AVAILABLE HERE
IN ANY EVENT, CORAL IT.
CORAL
SWING
LOW
SWEET
CHARIOT?
DETAILS OF ALL
INTERNATIONALS
AVAILABLE HERE
IN ANY EVENT, CORAL IT.
CORAL

Planet Kid's/Arena One

COUNTRY OF ORIGIN: United Kingdom
DESIGNER: Caroline Dibble, Alan Thompson/Fitch, London, England
DATE: 1995 June
TYPE OF IDENTITY IMPLEMENTATION: Complete identity
TARGET AUDIENCE: Children and their parents
CLIENT'S BRIEF: To provide a unique and fun environment for the children's market, to include an indoor playground, food outlets, a cinema and parent's lounge. To offer an exciting, escapist adventure area, to balance active play with interactive learning whilst communicating to children on a level they understand
DESIGN RATIONALE: The experience begins at the reception area, with its padded video walls and bright colour scheme. From here children enter the major play zone – NRG Box – through their very own obstacle tunnel. The NRG Box is a large 380m, double height play area, with room for over 200 children, which comprises colourful play equipment such as slides, climbing frames, tunnels and ball pits. Around the side of the room, interactive games provide an opportunity for children to play with educational toys such as computer paint boxes and interactive musical instruments. Nearby, a toddler zone, with small scale climbing frame and soft play equipment offers equally enticing fun for the under fives. An adult lounge situated on a mezzanine above, allows parents to watch the children below. A set of fun characters; Spotnik the Dog and Bob the Bouncing Computer appear on signage and play points throughout. Clothing and educational material are merchandised and carry the Planet Kid's 'rocket' logo and characters
PHOTOGRAPHER: Chris Hollick
PROJECT DIRECTOR: John Harrison/Fitch

(continued on pp. 94-5)

EMERGENCY SLIDE
SLIDE

SUPERBOWL

Please don't bring food or drink in the play area!

Taunton

Bristol

Hollywood

COUNTRY OF ORIGIN: United Kingdom

DESIGNER: Graham Barton, Gary Ingram, Garrett Reil and Jeremy Vinson/Butler Cornfield Dedman, London, England

DATE: 1994 Autumn

TYPE OF IDENTITY IMPLEMENTATION: Complete identity

TARGET AUDIENCE: Primarily youth based audience

CLIENT'S BRIEF: To create a brand which is strong and flexible, engaging and amusing, clear and concise, confident and professional, energetic and alive and new and exciting

DESIGN RATIONALE: A giant 'h' icon was used to counter the anonymity of retail park sites. A simple lowercase 'h' was chosen so that it relies on its size and incongruity to be noticed. This is supplemented with a very simple 'hollywood' logotype and bold image graphics that personify the 'h' icon extended across a range of promotional material thus giving ownership of the 'h' to the company, its employees and customers

MODELMAKER: Mark Plenderleith

PHOTOGRAPHER: Simon Pugh

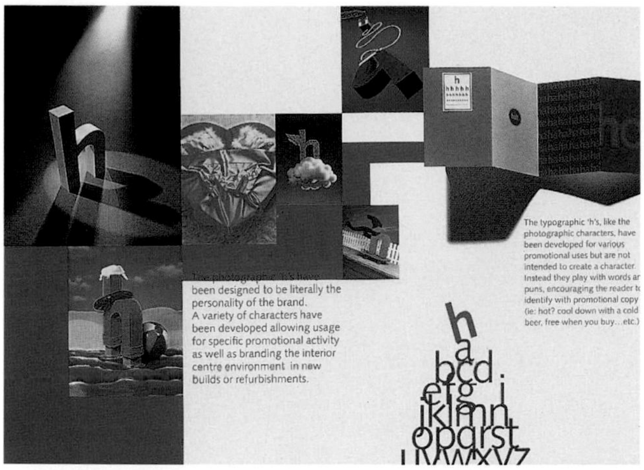
been designed to be literally the personality of the brand. A variety of characters have been developed allowing usage for specific promotional activity as well as branding the interior centre environment in new builds or refurbishments.
The typographic 'h's, like the photographic characters, have been developed for various promotional uses but are not intended to create a character. Instead they play with words and puns, encouraging the reader to identify with promotional copy (ie: hot? cool down with a cold beer, free when you buy...etc.)

hollywood
hollywood bowl
The logotypes should always be afforded their own space and due respect. However these principles must not make the identity look old or staid.
The logotypes may run up or down the page as appropriate.
Attention must always be paid to legibility.
The logotypes should never appear more than once on any page or sign.
hollywood bowl
hollywood bowl

abcdefghijkln
Syntax Ror
Syntax Italic abcdefghijklmnopqrstvw
1234567890
The new brand identity has various visual components which allow the flexibility to tailor promotions, signage or packaging to individual case requirements whilst maintaining the brand values and high standards across the wide variety of applications.
nopqrstuvw
Syntax Bold abcde fghijk lmnop qrstuv wxyz
1234567890
hollywoo

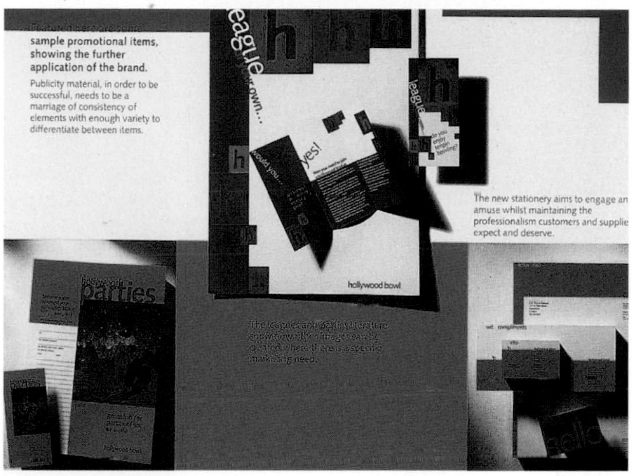
sample promotional items, showing the further application of the brand.
Publicity material, in order to be successful, needs to be a marriage of consistency of elements with enough variety to differentiate between items.
The new stationery aims to engage and amuse whilst maintaining the professionalism customers and suppliers expect and deserve.
yes!
parties
hollywood bowl

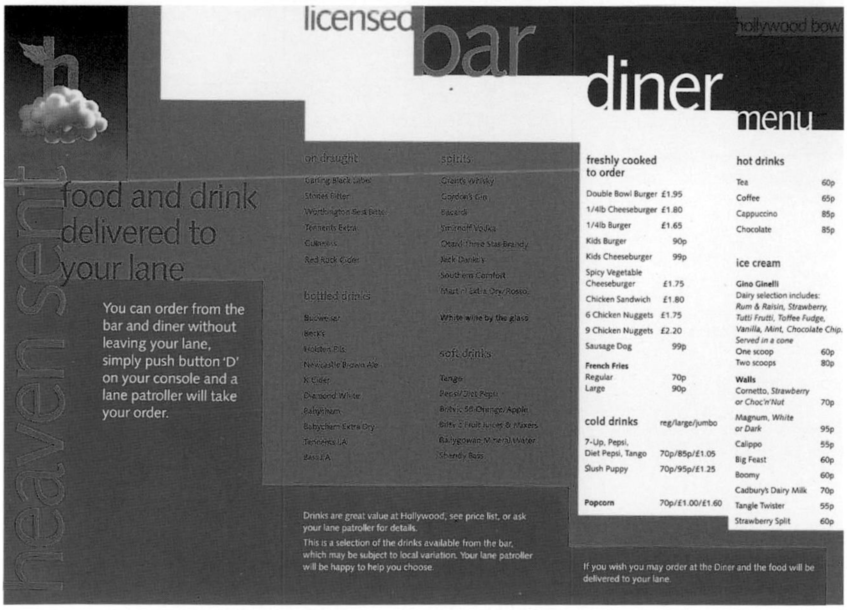
licensed
bar
diner
menu
hollywood bowl
heaven sent
food and drink delivered to your lane
You can order from the bar and diner without leaving your lane, simply push button 'D' on your console and a lane patroller will take your order.
on draught
spirits
bottled drinks
soft drinks
freshly cooked to order
Double Bowl Burger £1.95
1/4lb Cheeseburger £1.80
1/4lb Burger £1.65
Kids Burger 90p
Kids Cheeseburger 99p
Spicy Vegetable Cheeseburger £1.75
Chicken Sandwich £1.80
6 Chicken Nuggets £1.75
9 Chicken Nuggets £2.20
Sausage Dog 99p
French Fries
Regular 70p
Large 90p
cold drinks reg/large/jumbo
7-Up, Pepsi, Diet Pepsi, Tango 70p/85p/£1.05
Slush Puppy 70p/95p/£1.25
Popcorn 70p/£1.00/£1.60
hot drinks
Tea 60p
Coffee 65p
Cappuccino 85p
Chocolate 85p
ice cream
Gino Ginelli
Dairy selection includes: Rum & Raisin, Strawberry, Tutti Frutti, Toffee Fudge, Vanilla, Mint, Chocolate Chip. Served in a cone
One scoop 60p
Two scoops 80p
Walls
Cornetto, Strawberry or Choc'n'Nut 70p
Magnum, White or Dark 95p
Calippo 55p
Big Feast 60p
Boomy 60p
Cadbury's Dairy Milk 70p
Tangle Twister 55p
Strawberry Split 60p
Drinks are great value at Hollywood, see price list, or ask your lane patroller for details.
This is a selection of the drinks available from the bar, which may be subject to local variation. Your lane patroller will be happy to help you choose.
If you wish you may order at the Diner and the food will be delivered to your lane.

Big Future

COUNTRY OF ORIGIN: America

DESIGNER: Theresa Henrekin/AIA and Jim Keane, Jane McNeely, Rich Nelson, Gen Obata/Kiku Obata & Company, St. Louis, Missouri, USA

DATE: 1994 December

TYPE OF IDENTITY IMPLEMENTATION: Overall concept, identity, store design, visual merchandising, signage and interactive game kiosks

TARGET AUDIENCE: Children 4–18 and their parents

CLIENT'S BRIEF: To create an entertaining environment with more than 80 exciting and futuristic adventures such as virtual reality and high-tech video games. Interactive experiences, a themed playground area for young children, a snack bar and an extensive gift shop had to be included in the site

DESIGN RATIONALE: The design of Big Future creates a unique, non-violent interactive environment for children. The 'outside' play area is designed for younger children. It features a climbing volcano with red lava slides, a seventeen-platform tree-house, a giant ant farm and a two storey rocket ship. The 'inside' is a series of colourful spaces with various interactive adventures for older children

FIXTURE FABRICATORS: Design Fabricators, USA

PHOTOGRAPHER: Alise O'Brien

SIGNAGE FABRICATORS: Engravings Unlimited, USA

CHILL

IN
FUEL

Music
PEACE
IN
Guitar

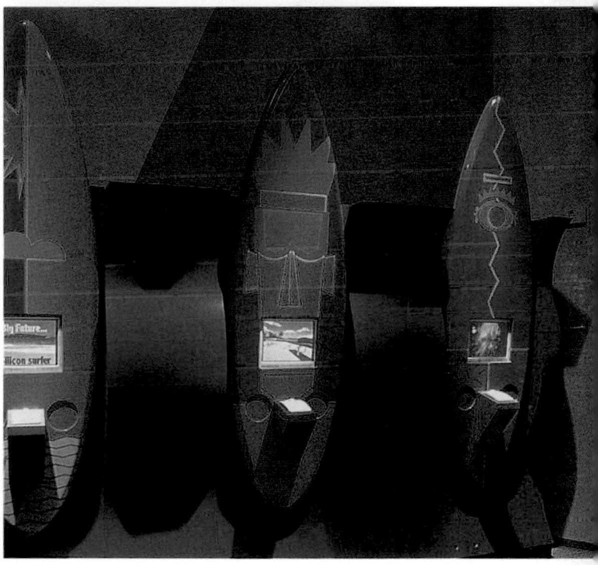

JAM

FASHION

4

Levi's Flagship Store, Regent's Street

COUNTRY OF ORIGIN: United Kingdom

DESIGNER: Checkland Kindleysides Design Ltd, England

DATE: 1994

TYPE OF IDENTITY IMPLEMENTATION: Shop fascia, interior and exterior, internal signage, packaging

TARGET AUDIENCE: General public

CLIENT'S BRIEF: To create a theatre like atmosphere and provide customers with the definitive Levi's experience, drawing on the hundred and forty years history of one of the world's oldest clothing brands. (The flagship is the first company owned Original Levi Store in the world). To maintain Levi's number one brand status, provide a strong and contemporary product showcase and raise the bar on visual excellence

DESIGN RATIONALE: The flagship design achieves a balance; retail store, brand archive and gallery. The entrance area positions Levi's as the Original Jeans featuring the oldest pair owned by the company. At 1,000 square feet this area provides a theatre for the brand in which large scale displays and sets are created. Further inside the Levi's story is told in history modules each designed to portray a milestone in the brand's development using authentic props and multimedia. The first of its kind, The Fit Centre carries every permutation of Levi's size and is fitted with over 400 pairs of jeans, housed in individual drawers. The basement, 1,000 square feet, is dedicated to the gallery which shows the work of artists as well as previewing new Levi's commercials

(continued on pp.106/7)

S.F. CA
The Birth of the
Girls Original
Girls Original
Original

LEVI STRAUSS & CO.
ORIGINAL RIVETED

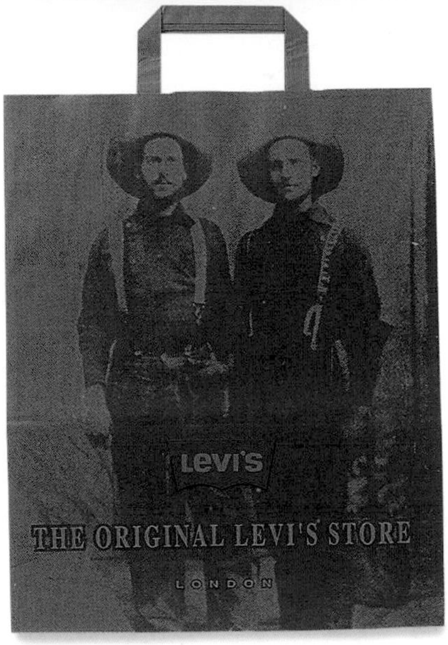
Levi's
THE ORIGINAL LEVI'S STORE
LONDON

ORIGINAL RIVETED
PATENTED IN U.S.
THE ORIGINAL JEANS
SINCE 1850
LEVI STRAUSS & CO.
SAN FRANCISCO CAL.
ORIGINAL
PATENTED IN U.S.
ORIGINAL
LEVI'S
STORE

THE ORIGINAL JEANS
SINCE 1850
LEVI'S

Store card

Sticker

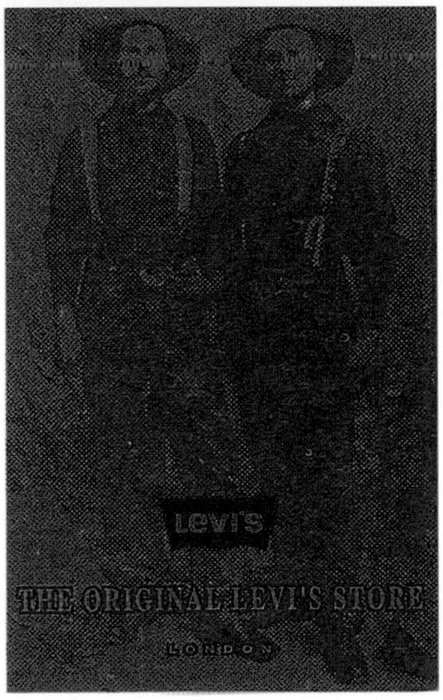

Label

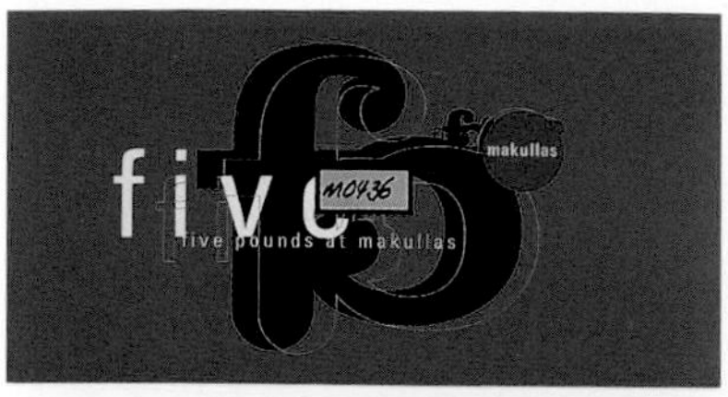
five
M0436
five pounds at makullas
makullas

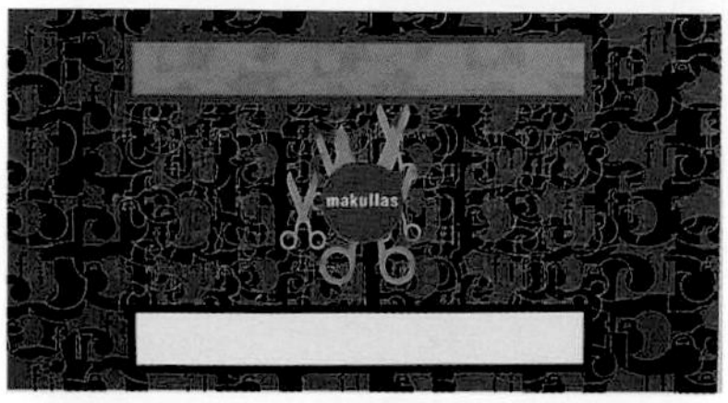
makullas

makullas
one hundred pounds at makullas
one
hundred

makullas
1030

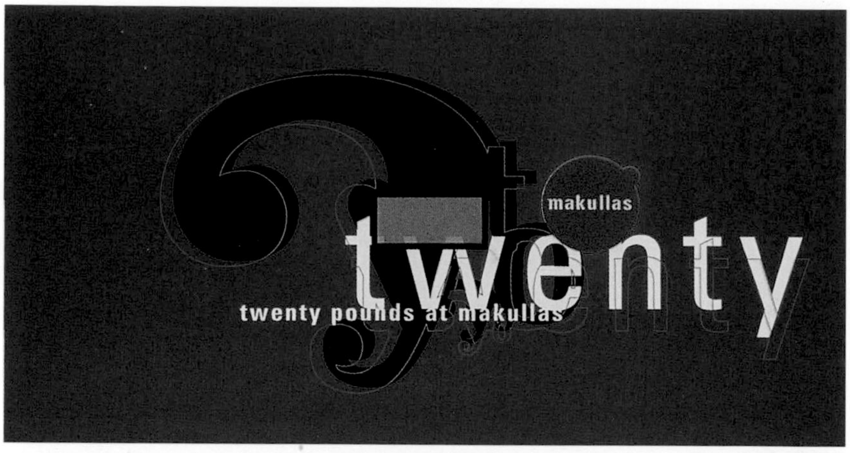
makullas
twenty
twenty pounds at makullas

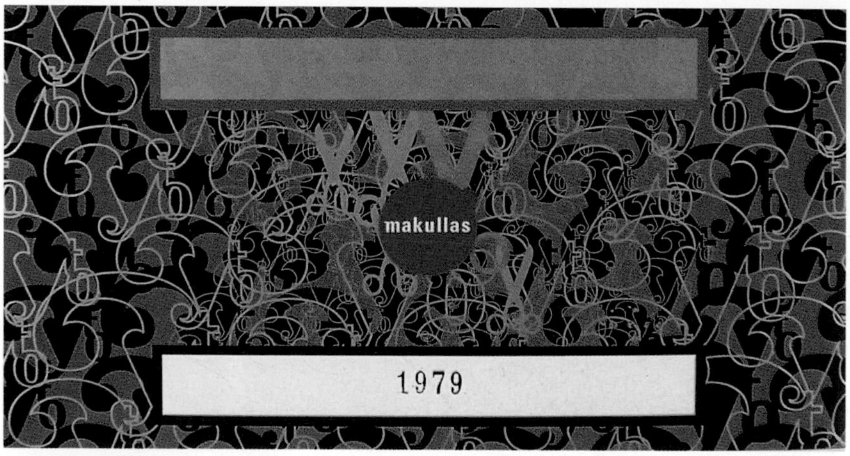
makullas
1979

makullas

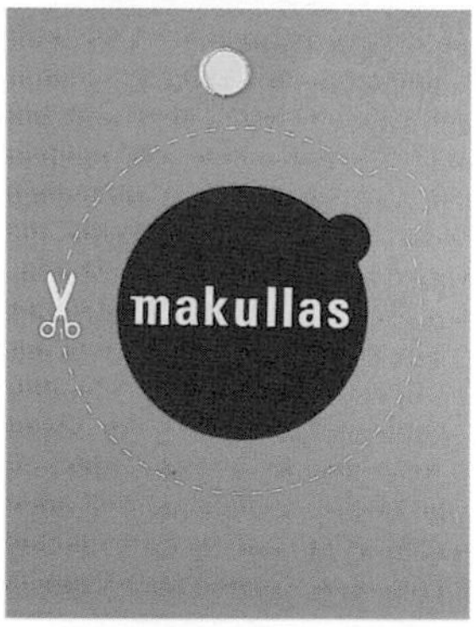
makullas

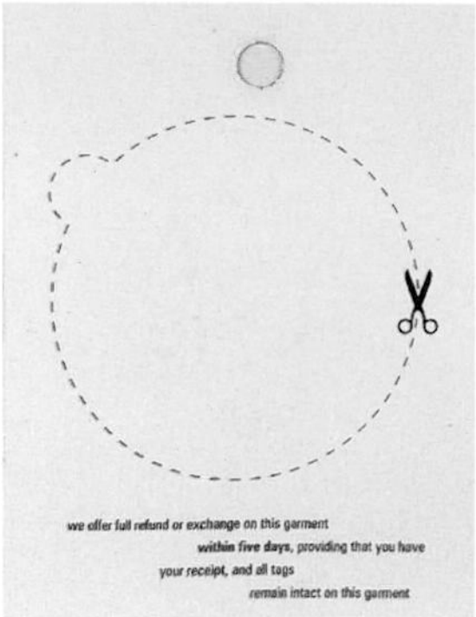
we offer full refund or exchange on this garment
within five days, providing that you have
your receipt, and all tags
remain intact on this garment

makullas

Makullas

COUNTRY OF ORIGIN: The Republic of Ireland
DESIGNER: Niall Sweeney
DATE: 1994 March
TYPE OF IDENTITY IMPLEMENTATION: Stationery, carrier bags, tokens, shop fascia, interior
TARGET AUDIENCE: Young, fashion conscious Dubliners
CLIENT'S BRIEF: To open a shop in a wholly unique environment with an emphasis on unique quality product and service
DESIGN RATIONALE: The building was architecturally reinstated as a landmark, with huge central doors, large open spaces, mezzanines, and the most dynamic of modern Interiors. The name is derived from 'McCullogh's', the site's previous name. Large symbolic roundels formed the core of the design, from the logo to the signage, and great importance is put on design and typographic detail, even on the 'grassy' bag, silver stickered bag and scissored sky
ART DIRECTOR: Frank Stanley/Makullas

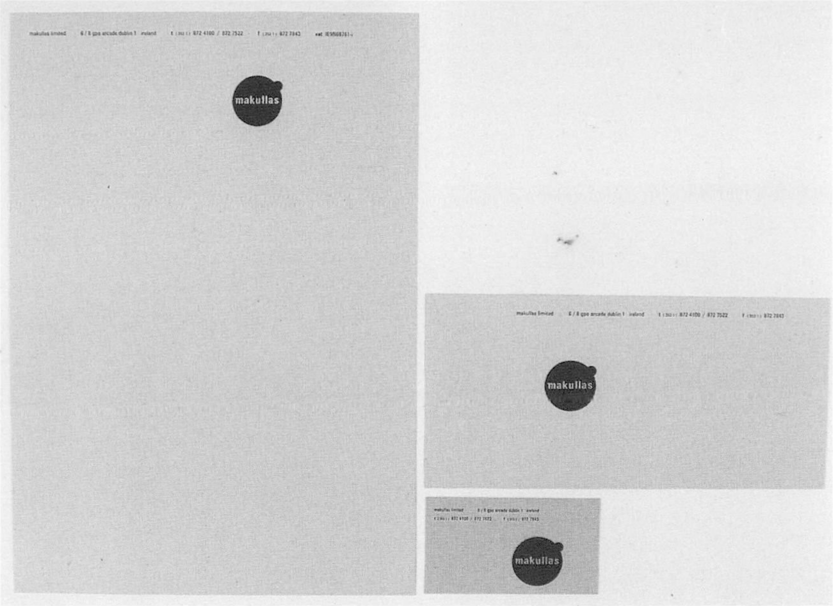

Subzero at Lanalgo LDA

COUNTRY OF ORIGIN: Portugal

DESIGNER: Ria Dakin-Potts, Richard Hill/Marketplace Design Partnership, Abingdon, Oxon, England

DATE: 1993

TYPE OF IDENTITY IMPLEMENTATION: Interior design supported by leaflets and posters displayed outside the department store and as 'statement stutters' to store card customers

TARGET AUDIENCE: 18–25 year olds

CLIENT'S BRIEF: To redesign the basement area with poor trading performance into a new retail concept

DESIGN RATIONALE: Innovative designs for both the interior and graphics were employed to appeal to the target audience, and resulted in an increase in annual turnover and improved cash flow. This enabled the store to stock high quality premium priced items

La Buandrie at Voyage

COUNTRY OF ORIGIN: United Kingdom

DESIGNER: Teresa Roviras

DATE: 1995 March

TYPE OF IDENTITY IMPLEMENTATION: Logo, carrier bag, swing tags, woven labels

TARGET AUDIENCE: Those in search of originality and individuality

CLIENT'S BRIEF: To create a spacious and light environment inspired by the concept of a French laundry room, as a backdrop to a collection of predominantly white clothes and raw fabrics

DESIGN RATIONALE: Following the idea of the laundry, the graphics are simple and functional, using ready made brown carrier bags overprinted with bold pristine white type with hand applied bamboo handles. Clothes pegs are used to fasten 'crisp' glassine bags and a 'white wash' image for the swing tickets has been applied

ARCHITECT: Spencer Fung, England

PHOTOGRAPHY: Andreas Schmidt

LA BUANDRIE

Ted Baker

COUNTRY OF ORIGIN: United Kingdom
DESIGNER: Harper Mackay Ltd, London, England
DATE: 1988
TYPE OF IDENTITY IMPLEMENTATION: Entire retail concept
TARGET AUDIENCE: Men aged between 16–35 years
CLIENT'S BRIEF: To create an individual shopping atmosphere in which the customer could shop at ease. To enhance the qualities offered by the Baker myth by giving a simple, uncluttered enclosure for the display of free-standing furniture and merchandise
DESIGN RATIONALE: 'Ted' is based on the apotheosis of pre-war gentlemanly charm. Natural, traditional materials were chosen for their inherent tactile qualities and colour; riven slate, hewn from quarries; metalwork, wrought from the foundry, hand finished with care and precision were amalgamated to give monolithic presence to the Ted Baker interior. Each site has been taken as an individual unit with its own inherent characteristics and where possible the designs have been moulded around the existing architectural structure

(continued on pp.116-7)

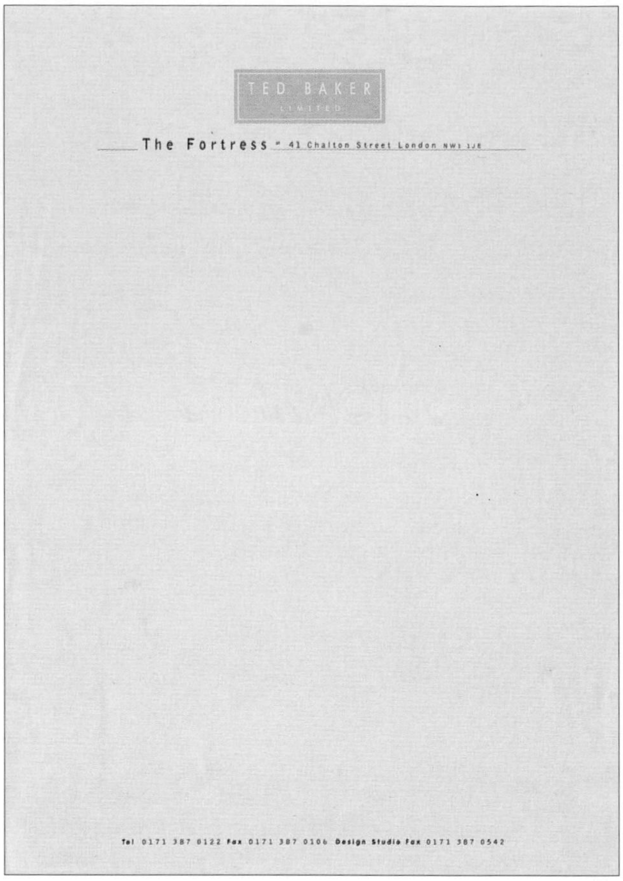

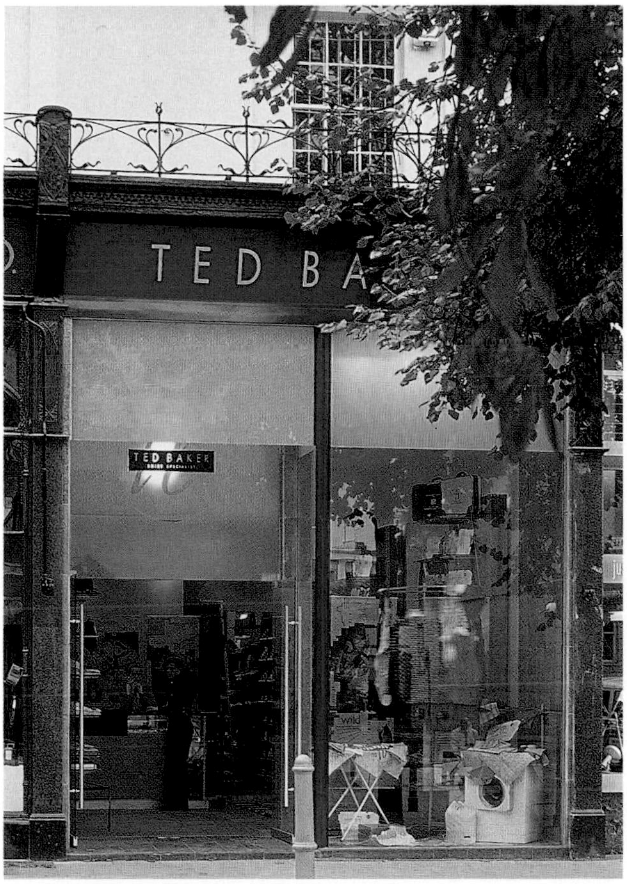

Cheltenham

Sheffield

Covent Garden

NEWS RELEASE
"Collar and cuffs which bore the ineffacable signs of dirty laundry reflect the shadow of impending disaster."
TED BAKER

3
wild
4
travel
planes
trains and boats and planes
boats
wild
TED BAKER
trains and boats and planes
took
you
away
wild thing.
you make
everything groovy.
TED BAKER
travel

TED BAKER

Duke Street

Horne Brothers plc

COUNTRY OF ORIGIN: United Kingdom

DESIGNER: David Vickery/The Jenkins Group, London, England

DATE: 1992 Spring

TYPE OF IDENTITY IMPLEMENTATION: All elements

TARGET AUDIENCE: Male 30+, aspirational and discerning – 'mid budget'

CLIENT'S BRIEF: In line with Horne's new marketing strategy, Jenkins had to design an image with broad appeal concentrating on quality environment, to make shopping easy and comfortable

DESIGN RATIONALE: The scheme was conceived around classic, simple and unpretentious detailing with materials selected for their honesty and inherent longevity. The steel is satin finished and solid oak fixtures are oiled. Colour is added via painted walls and carpeting, allowing the respective environments to develop their own lasting appeal

HORNE
BROTHERS

Leeds

HORNE
BROTHERS
WOMAN
HORNE
BROTHERS
HORNE
BROTHERS
HORNE
BROTHERS
WOMAN

Fosters

COUNTRY OF ORIGIN: United Kingdom
DESIGNER: John Herbert, Brian Rutherford, Taj Wilkinson/John Herbert Partnership, London, England
DATE: 1994 September
TYPE OF IDENTITY IMPLEMENTATION: Fascia, store interior, internal signage, bags, stationery
TARGET AUDIENCE: 15–35 year old men
CLIENT'S BRIEF: To break away from Foster's tradition of selling suits and simple basics and to establish 'Fosters Trading Company' as the fashionable destination for men's jeans and casual clothing
DESIGN RATIONALE: To create a trading identity and environment with a masculine contemporary and casual ambience. The use of natural materials on the signage and throughout, emphasises the real authority in selection and quality
PHOTOGRAPHER: Jon O'Brien
SIGN MAKER: Original Sand Blasted Sign Company

CREATING THE RIGHT ENVIRONMENT
FOSTERS
TRADING COMPANY
FOSTERS
TRADING COMPANY
WITH COMPLIMENTS
STAY COOL THIS SUMMER
A NEW ERA OF SUCCESS

FOSTERS
TRADING COMPANY
Lee

Suit Direct

COUNTRY OF ORIGIN: United Kingdom
DESIGNER: Julian Davies, Adam Knapp, Karen McGary/ Sears Davies Ltd, London, England
DATE: 1995 October
TYPE OF IDENTITY IMPLEMENTATION: All internal signage, ticketing, display graphics, promotional banners, leaflets
TARGET AUDIENCE: Male 20–50 years
CLIENT'S BRIEF: To design and produce an identity for a new retail chain of menswear shops offering unbeatable value on a wide selection of 'famous name' tailored garments
DESIGN RATIONALE: A striking visual identity (including name generation) was developed. It is capable of a variety of applications appealing to a wide age group and is very memorable. The logo upholds the client's proposition – style at unbeatable prices
INTERIOR DESIGNER: Marvin Shane/Tilney Lumsden Shane, England
PHOTOGRAPHER: Peter Dazeley
STYLIST: John Parkin

(continued on pp.124/5)

fitting
ROOMS

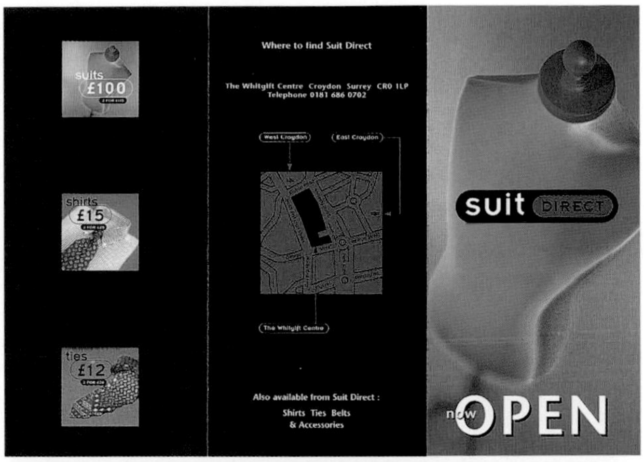
suits
£100
shirts
£15
ties
£12
Where to find Suit Direct
The Whitgift Centre Croydon Surrey CR0 1LP
Telephone 0181 686 0702
West Croydon
East Croydon
The Whitgift Centre
Also available from Suit Direct :
Shirts Ties Belts
& Accessories
suit DIRECT
now OPEN

PRICE PROMISE
Welcome to Suit Direct
We guarantee you unbeatable prices on a unique collection of fine branded tailoring
If you can buy the same garment cheaper elsewhere we'll refund the difference
Take advantage of our innovative "two for" offers and save even more!
suit DIRECT
All Suits
DIRECT PRICE
TWO FOR PRICE
£100 £175
£125 £225
£150 £265
£175 £310
£200 £350
OPENING OFFER
Free shirt
when you buy any suit
Choose a free shirt from a selected range including
Pierre Cardin & Ben Sherman

suit DIRECT

GIARDINO
Hello ..... is anybody there?
What do you mean, opening soon !?!
I thought they said August !!!
This year or next !!!
Hurry up, I've a meeting at 11
opening
Thursday
5th October
11.00am
SUi

CAFÉ GIARDINO
saw som
I know you'
…irt on !!!
opening
Thursday
5th October
11.00am
RECT
ple-e-e-e-ase !!!
what ?!? … come back next week !

Ballantyne Cashmere

COUNTRY OF ORIGIN: Scotland

DESIGNER: Caroline Schroder/Landor Associates, London, England

DATE: 1990 October

TYPE OF IDENTITY IMPLEMENTATION: Signage, stationery, fascia, bags, internal decor

TARGET AUDIENCE: European high earners and the Far East

CLIENT'S BRIEF: To build greater brand recognition for Ballantyne in all its markets worldwide whilst differentiating the company on the basis of its products' quality

DESIGN RATIONALE: The hand drawn 'B' symbol was used to crystallise the qualities of Ballantyne Cashmere. The design also established an application system for the identity emphasising the hand-crafted, tactile nature of the company's Cashmere products. This feature was strongly reflected throughout the application of its identity, and is emphasised in the subtle hues in the water colouring of the 'B' mark, in the gold graphic element and in the handmade paper that carries the identity on many of its applications

ADDITIONAL CREDITS: Richard Ford/Landor Associates

BALLANTYNE
Cashmere

BALLANTYNE

BALLANTYNE
Cashmere
Stephanie Curtis
Merchandise Executive
The Ballantyne Cashmere Company Limited
4-6 Savile Row, London WIX IAF
Tel (0171) 734 2861 Fax (0171) 494 1613

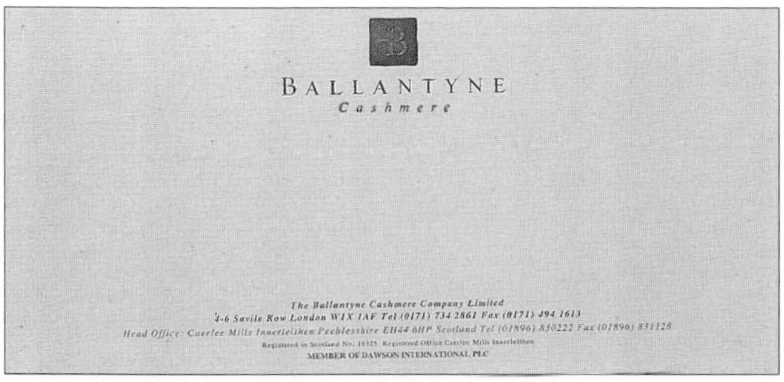
BALLANTYNE
Cashmere
The Ballantyne Cashmere Company Limited
4-6 Savile Row London WIX IAF Tel (0171) 734 2861 Fax (0171) 494 1613
Head Office: Caerlee Mills Innerleithen Peeblesshire EH44 6HP Scotland Tel (01896) 830222 Fax (01896) 831128
MEMBER OF DAWSON INTERNATIONAL PLC

BALLANTYNE
Cashmere
The Ballantyne Cashmere Company Limited
Caerlee Mills Innerleithen Peeblesshire EH44 6HP Scotland Tel (0896) 830222 Fax (0896) 831128 Telex 72185
London Office: 4-6 Savile Row WIX IAF Tel (071) 734 2861 Fax (071) 494 1613

BALLANTYNE
Cashmere

HOME

CUSTOMER SERVICES
PLEASE PAY HERE
CHILDRENSWEAR

PLEASE PAY HERE
Womenswear
Womenswear

Bhs

COUNTRY OF ORIGIN: United Kingdom
DESIGNER: 20/20 Design & Stretgy Consultants, London, England
DATE: 1995 April
TYPE OF IDENTITY IMPLEMENTATION: Complete identity
TARGET AUDIENCE: The family focused working woman who demands quality and mainstream fashion at competitive prices

CLIENT'S BRIEF: To develop a new Bhs store concept that responds to the needs of the Bhs target shopper. To give Bhs customers the confidence to shop across the entire store - allowing access to the Bhs buying team's total vision, the latest looks and departmental offers. To be flexible to allow for seasonal changes
DESIGN RATIONALE: Mini stage areas or 'epicentres' - one for each Bhs merchandise division were introduced, each with its own distinct division specific personality. A new trading identity was implemented for the Bhs business which is now being strategically introduced across the chain. At Cambridge, the new identity takes pride of place on the giant shopfront, giving the customer a snapshot of the whole Bhs store at a glance
PHOTOGRAPHER: Jon O'Brien

egg
egg
egg

Egg

COUNTRY OF ORIGIN: United Kingdom

DESIGNER: Michael Nash Associates, London, England

DATE: 1995 April

TYPE OF IDENTITY IMPLEMENTATION: Complete identity

TARGET AUDIENCE:Discerning females

CLIENT'S BRIEF:To provide a simple yet sophisticated llogo

DESIGN RATIONALE:Lower case lettering is used on all aspects of the packaging carrying the name 'egg'. The plain and elegant simplicity of this design echoes that of the merchandise and location

San Francisco Clothing

COUNTRY OF ORIGIN: America

DESIGNER: George Tscherny/George Tscherny Inc., New York City, New York, USA

TYPE OF IDENTITY IMPLEMENTATION: All elements

TARGET AUDIENCE: Women in their teens and twenties

CLIENT'S BRIEF: To produce a signature which echoes the pop/punk merchandise being offered to a young audience

DESIGN RATIONALE: The graffiti like signature was intended to separate the company from conventional clothing retailers

N.Y. LOVES S.F.
SALE
NOW!
SF
WOW!
SAN FRANCISCO
975 Lex
472·8740
CLOTHING

SF
SAN FRANCISCO CLOTHING

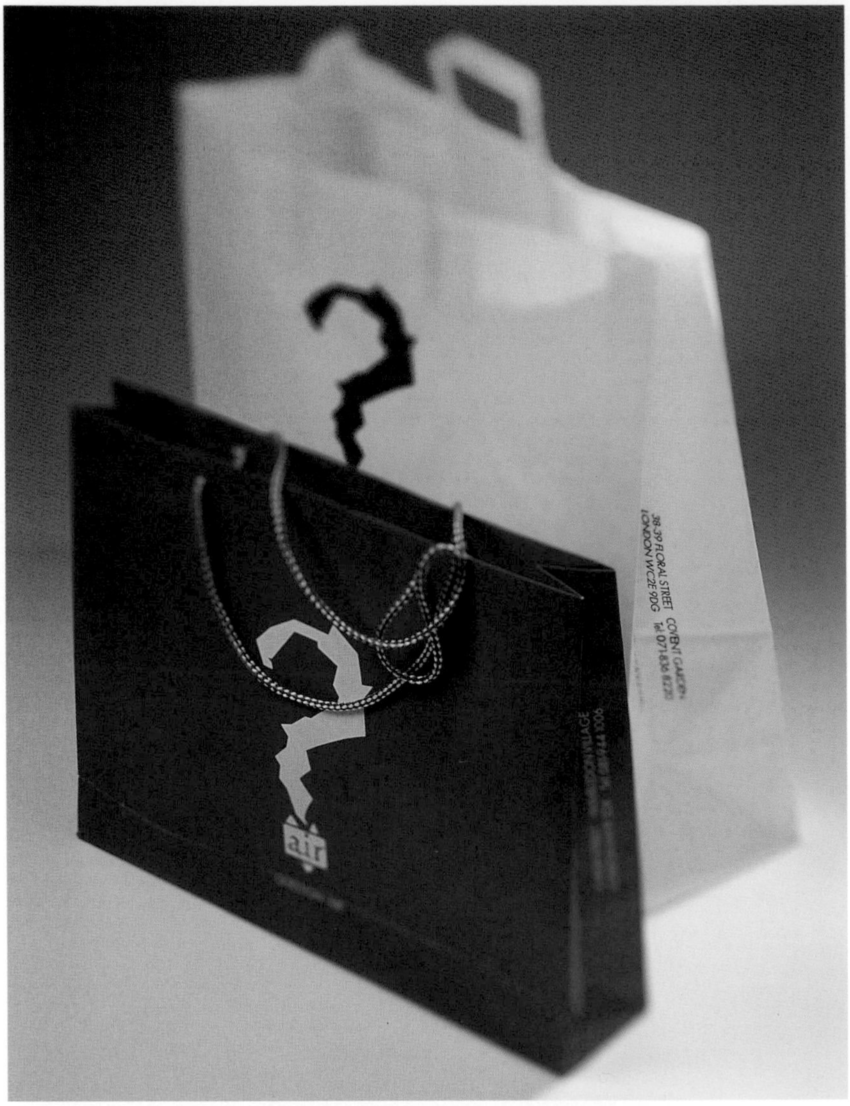

?Air

COUNTRY OF ORIGIN: United Kingdom

DESIGNER: Judy Ross/Ross and Ross, London, England

DATE: 1991 February

TYPE OF IDENTITY IMPLEMENTATION: Bags, stationery, fascia, editorials

TARGET AUDIENCE: Women between 18–80 years

CLIENT'S BRIEF: To create a catchy but unpretentious name and logo which would stick in the mind for its originality

DESIGN RATIONALE: Both the clothes and interior of the shop are used to convey an idea of familiarity but also of something different and exciting. The emphasis is on the clothes not the shop. It is more important for a customer to like the garments than the walls

ILLUSTRATORS: Students from St. Martin's Art College

exhibit

COUNTRY OF ORIGIN: Northern Ireland
DESIGNER: Mike Jewitt/Metropolis 88 Design Group, London, England
DATE: 1994 June
TYPE OF IDENTITY IMPLEMENTATION: All elements
TARGET AUDIENCE: Girls aged between 15–22 years
CLIENT'S BRIEF: To develop a new corporate identity which reflected the materials and current fashion trends. To be flexible to enable application to any product, garment or other retail aspect
DESIGN RATIONALE: Having controlled the image and identity for exhibit over the last five years it was necessary to reflect the new fashion through the identity. Materials and colours are used to mimic materials used in today's clothes such as sand, bleached woods and stone

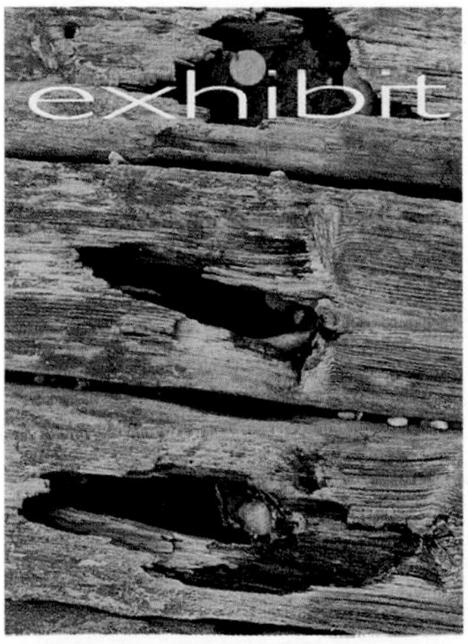

Foravi/Freebeat

COUNTRY OF ORIGIN: America

DESIGNER: Richard Goltry/Foravi Inc., New York, USA

TYPE OF IDENTITY IMPLEMENTATION: Complete identity including promotional items

TARGET AUDIENCE: Teenagers to the middle aged

CLIENT'S BRIEF: To design a logo to attract clients throughout the States, Europe and in particular Japan whilst remaining alternative and up-beat

DESIGN RATIONALE: Foravi/Freebeat is a wholesale operation based in Soho, New York, so to differentiate it from the rest about fifty per cent of the merchandise produced carries logos and graphics. The logo and garment designs are clean and sharp with an industrial edge

ADDITIONAL CREDITS: Devora Avikzer

FREE BEAT
FORAVI
FREE BEAT
MADE IN U.S.A.
SHOWROOM: 57•59 GREENE ST. SOHO, N.Y. 212 • 226 • 0041 FAX 212 • 431 • 3341

FORAVI
FREE BEAT

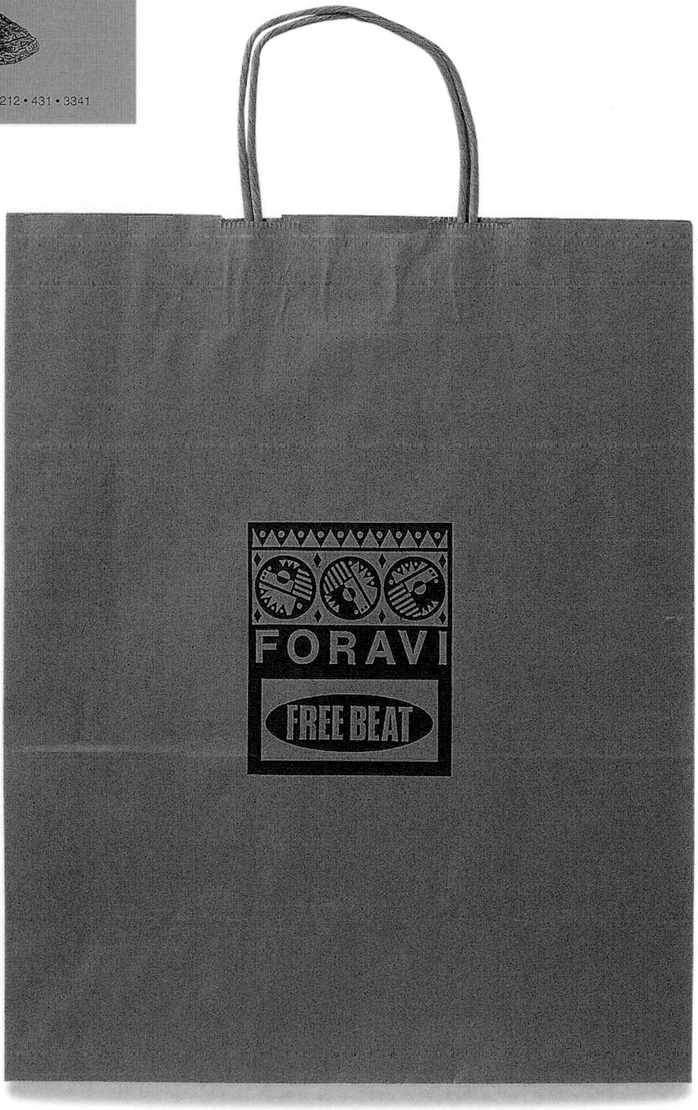
FORAVI
FREE BEAT

Luminous Blue at Voyage

COUNTRY OF ORIGIN: United Kingdom

DESIGNER: Kate Goode/The Trigger Foundation, London, England

DATE: 1993

TYPE OF IDENTITY IMPLEMENTATION: Complete identity; T-shirts, bags, logo, swing tags

TARGET AUDIENCE: The fashion conscious rich rock and roll followers and actors

CLIENT'S BRIEF: To create an identity to reflect the new label. To be highly innovative and sympathetic to the quality and design of the clothes

DESIGN RATIONALE: A stylish logo was developed to catch the eye of discerning shoppers. Highly modern and minimalist use of colour, shape, size and materials are employed, for example the transparent plastic garment tags

LUMINOUS BLUE
L
UMI
NOUS
BLUE
SW
3
LUMINOUS BLUE
115 FULHAM ROAD
AT VOYAGE

ally capellino

Please reply to
☐ Head Office: Ally Capellino Ltd. N I R Metropolitan Wharf Wapping Wall London E1 9SS Telephone 0171 488 9777 Fax 0171 488 9852
☐ PR and Sales: Soho Showroom 43/45 Beak Street Soho London W1R 3LE Telephone 0171 437 5700 Fax 0171 734 3321
☐ Retail Store: Ally Capellino Retail Ltd. 95 Wardour Street Soho London W1V 3TE Telephone 0171 494 0768 Fax 0171 287 3814
☐ Reg. Office: 92 New Cavendish Street London W1M 7FA Ally Capellino Ltd. reg no. 1695594 Ally Capellino Retail Ltd. reg no. 2255504 Group VAT no. 365 5558 22

ally capellino

N I R Metropolitan Wharf Wapping Wall London E1 9SS Telephone 071 488 9777 Fax 071 488 9852

WITH COMPLIMENTS

ally capellino

N I R Metropolitan Wharf Wapping Wall London E1 9SS Telephone 071 488 9777 **Fax 071 488 9852**

TO:

FROM:

DATE: SHEETS:

FAX MESSAGE

ally capellino

ALISON LLOYD
DESIGN DIRECTOR

■ **HEAD OFFICE:**
Ally Capellino Ltd
N I R Metropolitan Wharf
Wapping Wall London E1 9SS
Telephone 0171 488 9777
Fax 0171 488 9852

☐ PR AND SALES:
Soho Showroom
43/45 Beak Street Soho
London W1R 3LE
Telephone 0171 437 5700
Fax 0171 734 3321

☐ RETAIL STORE:
Ally Capellino Retail Ltd
95 Wardour Street Soho
London W1V 3TE
Telephone 0171 494 0768
Fax 0171 287 3814

ally capellino

NUALA BARKER
RETAIL MANAGER AND BUYER

☐ HEAD OFFICE:
Ally Capellino Ltd
N I R Metropolitan Wharf
Wapping Wall London E1 9SS
Telephone 0171 488 9777
Fax 0171 488 9852

☐ PR AND SALES:
Soho Showroom
43/45 Beak Street Soho
London W1R 3LE
Telephone 0171 437 5700
Fax 0171 734 3321

■ **RETAIL STORE:**
Ally Capellino Retail Ltd
95 Wardour Street Soho
London W1V 3TE
Telephone 0171 494 0768
Fax 0171 287 3814

ally capellino

TOM KONIG OPPENHEIMER
PUBLIC RELATIONS

☐ HEAD OFFICE:
Ally Capellino Ltd
N I R Metropolitan Wharf
Wapping Wall London E1 9SS
Telephone 0171 488 9777
Fax 0171 488 9852

■ **PR AND SALES:**
Soho Showroom
43/45 Beak Street Soho
London W1R 3LE
Telephone 0171 437 5700
Fax 0171 734 3321

☐ RETAIL STORE:
Ally Capellino Retail Ltd
95 Wardour Street Soho
London W1V 3TE
Telephone 0171 494 0768
Fax 0171 287 3814

Ally Capellino

COUNTRY OF ORIGIN: United Kingdom
DESIGNER: Nick Waters/Colour Box Design, York, England
DATE: 1990 August
TYPE OF IDENTITY IMPLEMENTATION: Bags, stationery, fascia, internal signage
TARGET AUDIENCE: Professional and media women, 25–50 year olds
CLIENT'S BRIEF: To reflect Ally Capellino's clean, modernised English character
DESIGN RATIONALE: Ally Capellino's signature was chosen as the logo and is present from office correspondence paper to T-shirts and promotional material
ART DIRECTOR: Jonathan Platt

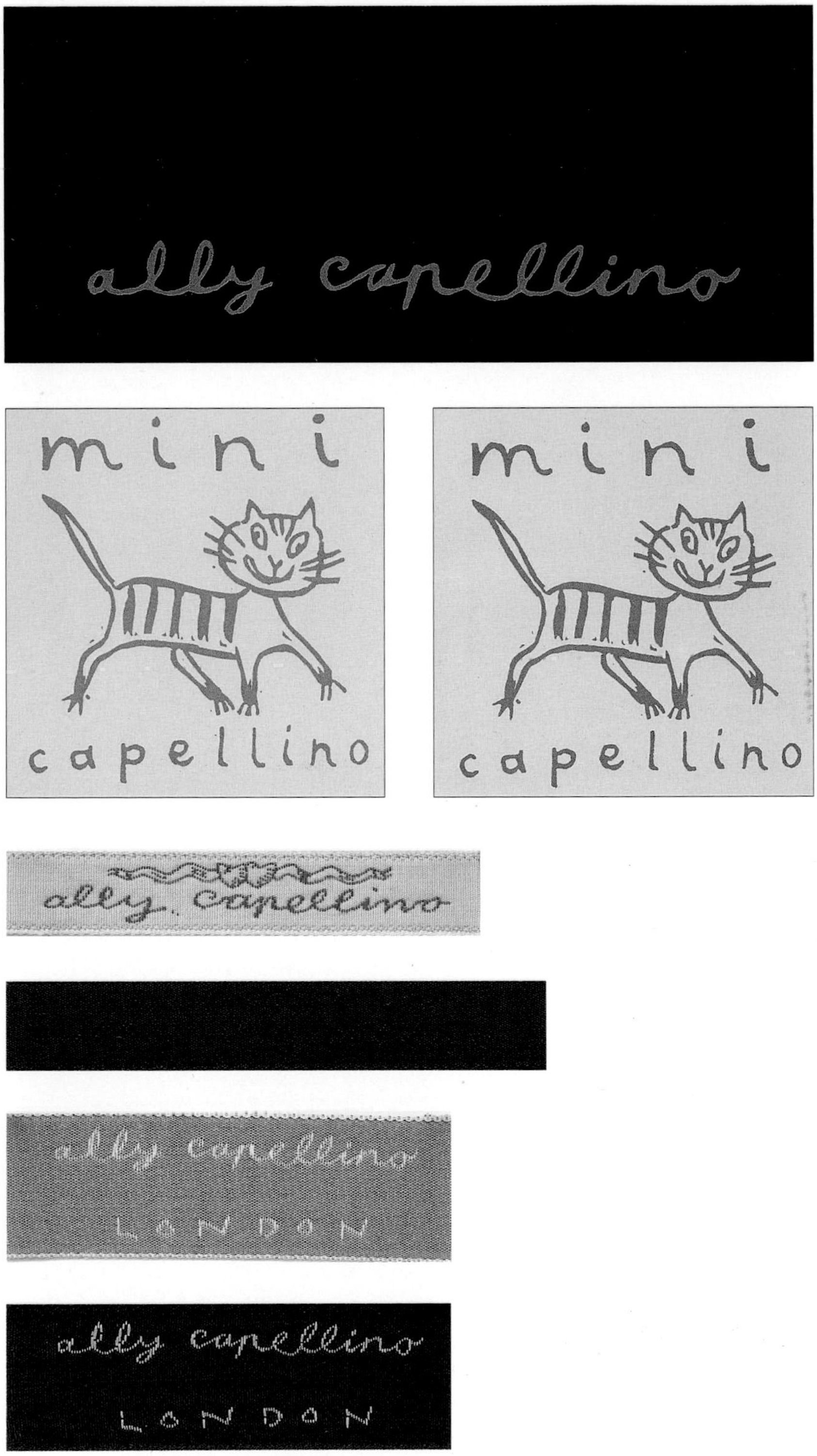

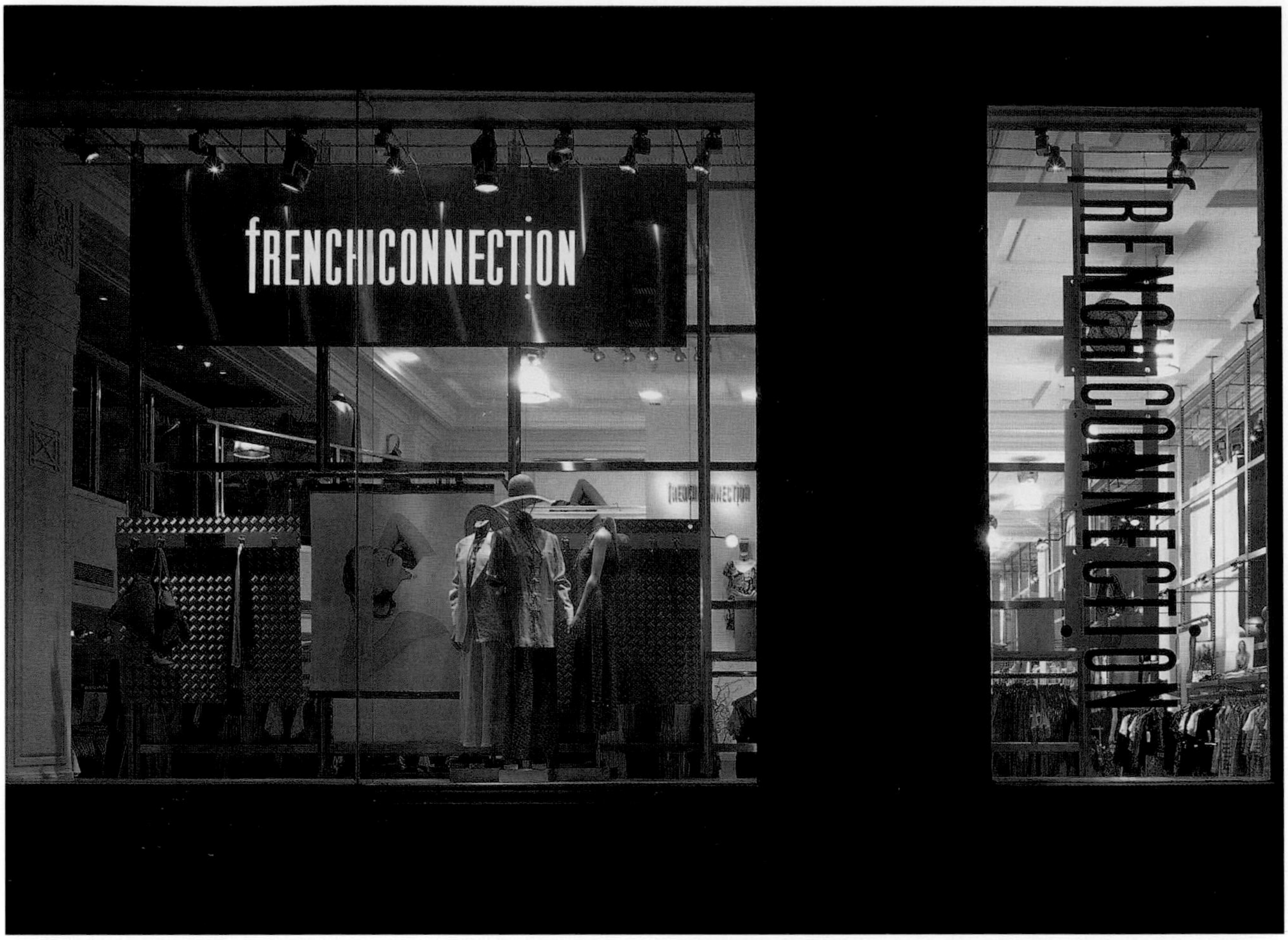

French Connection

COUNTRY OF ORIGIN: United Kingdom

DESIGNER: Valerie Wicks/DIN Graphics, London, England

DATE: 1993 August

TYPE OF IDENTITY IMPLEMENTATION: Bags

TARGET AUDIENCE: Young parents and children from 3–12 years

CLIENT'S BRIEF: To create a bag that can be practical and fun, to be used time and time again. To be in keeping with the French Connection children's identity

DESIGN RATIONALE: The bag was created around the existing swing ticket we had created earlier which used string colours and cut outs. The cut outs are transparent and a draw string duffle bag was designed which is easy for children to carry

(continued on pp.144-5)

FRENCH CONNECTION

FRENCH CONNECTION

FRENCH CONNECTION
MENSWEAR

FRENCH CONNECTION

FRENCH CONNECTION

28.3

RippelSteins

COUNTRY OF ORIGIN: America

DESIGNER: John Rippel and David Moreno, Santa Fe, USA

DATE: 1994 August

TYPE OF IDENTITY IMPLEMENTATION: Complete identity

TARGET AUDIENCE: Sophisticated professionals, European travellers, entertainment and art industry clients

CLIENT'S BRIEF: To feature merchandise previously unavailable in the Southwest and feature belts and sterling jewellery designed by John Rippel

DESIGN RATIONALE: The merchandising is designed to lead the customer through the store, offering a variety of options at every turn. A product mix merges masculine furnishings, fashion and personal accessories with tightly focused fashion collections – all with a commitment to lasting quality and longevity of design

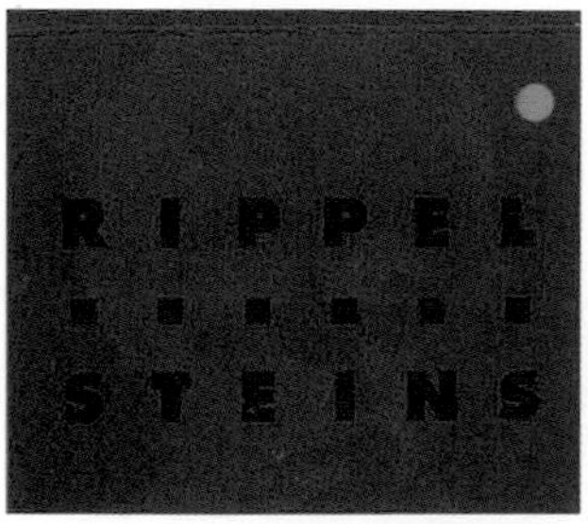

As a boy, you tried running away from home.
Today, a business trip is
as adventurous
as you get...
RIPPEL
STEINS

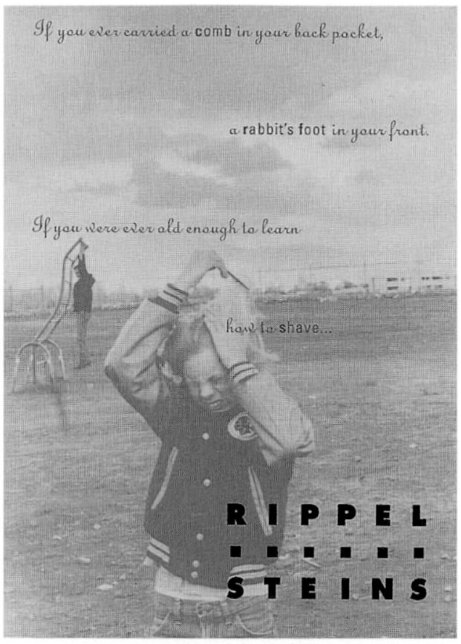
If you ever carried a comb in your back pocket,
a rabbit's foot in your front.
If you were ever old enough to learn
how to shave...
RIPPEL
STEINS

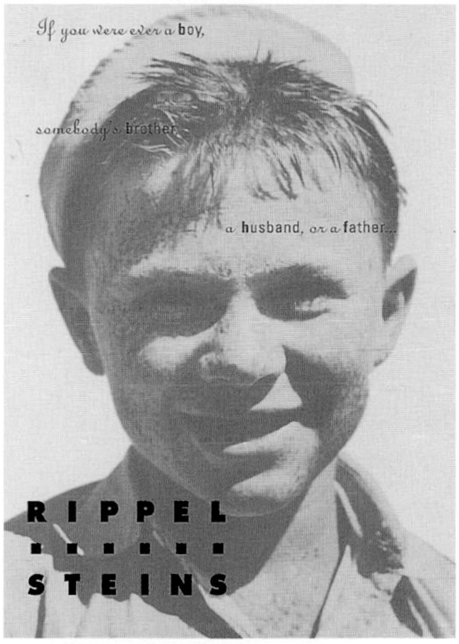
If you were ever a boy,
somebody's brother,
a husband, or a father...
RIPPEL
STEINS

130
west
water
street
santa
fe
new
mexico
87501
RIPPEL
STEINS

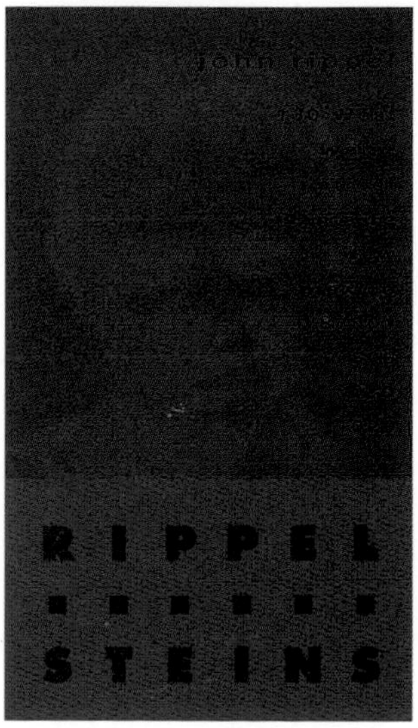
RIPPEL
STEINS

Armani Exchange

COUNTRY OF ORIGIN: America
DESIGNER: Giorgio Armani and Naomi Leff & Associates Inc., New York, USA
DATE: 1991 December
TYPE OF IDENTITY IMPLEMENTATION: Complete identity
TARGET AUDIENCE: High income bracket customers
CLIENT'S BRIEF: To attract the existing clientèle and encourage a potential new customer pool
DESIGN RATIONALE: Most elements of the packaging carry the AIX; a simple, unpretentious abbreviation which creates a visual impact. The stylish wrapping paper (seen opposite) is an example of the impact the Armani design without carrying the logo

(continued on pp.150-1)

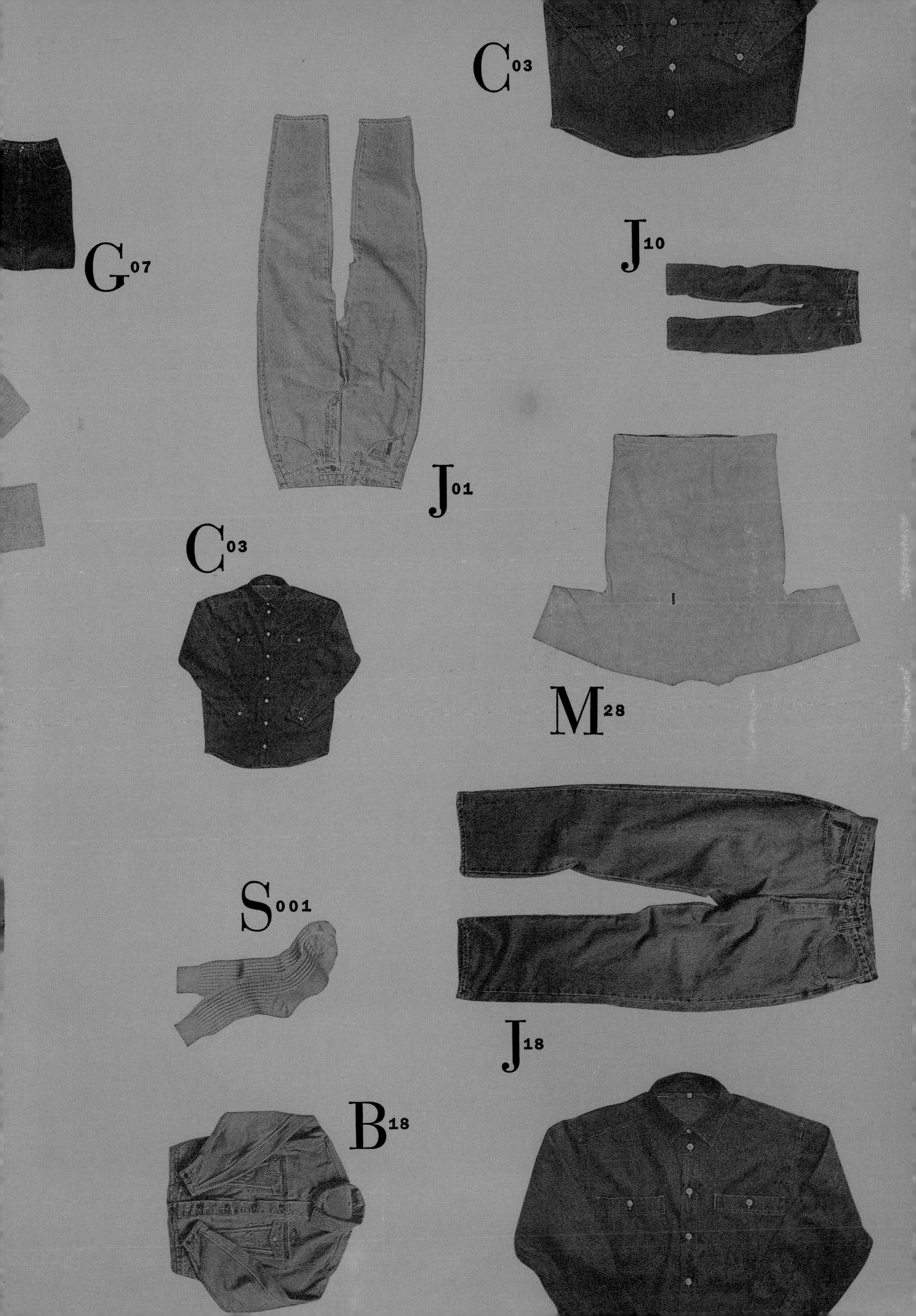
C03
G07
J10
J01
C03
M28
S001
J18
B18

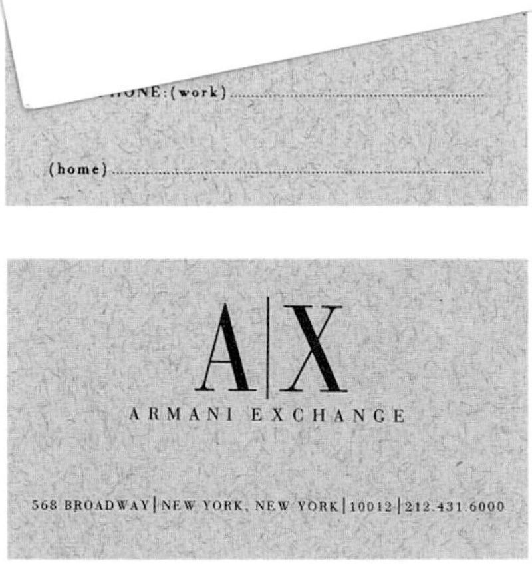

Above: Stickers

taly

Fornari, Roberto Pia/Art Force S.R.L.,

, Italy

ATE: 1993–1994

TYPE OF IDENTITY IMPLEMENTATION: Labelling

TARGET AUDIENCE: Children

CLIENT'S BRIEF: To offer an alternative to the fashion catalogue

DESIGN RATIONALE: The label for the jeans was 'Grant'. Using various sizes and shapes, the logo was implemented to differentiate from market leaders whilst attracting the fashion conscious teenager

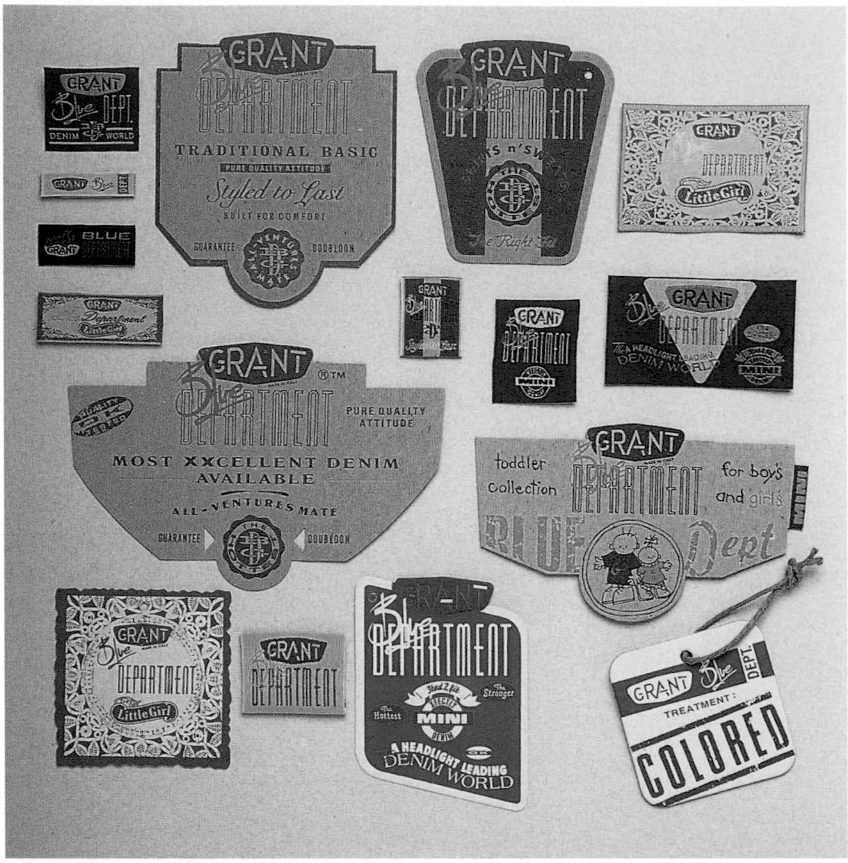

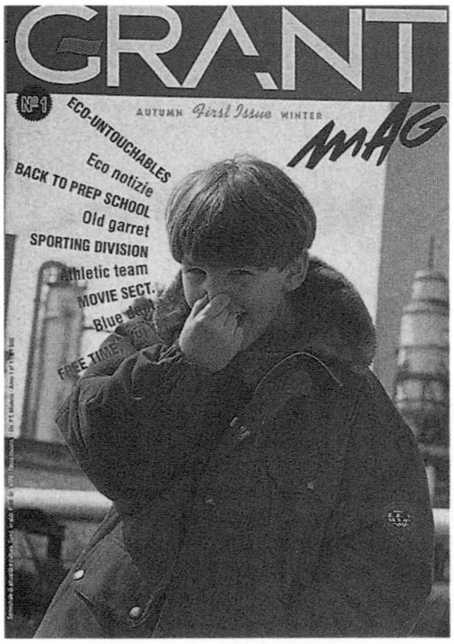

GRANT
Blue
DEPARTMENT
The Stronger
The Hottest
EVERY KID'S DREAM

Oilily
Oilily

Oilily

COUNTRY OF ORIGIN: The Netherlands

DESIGNER: Pam Bliss, Sylvia Teng/AIA, USA and Jim Keane/Kiku Obata & Co, St. Louis, Missouri, USA

DATE: 1994 October

TYPE OF IDENTITY IMPLEMENTATION: All elements

TARGET AUDIENCE: Women and children

CLIENT'S BRIEF: To design a store incorporating colourful, ethnic and patterned clothing

DESIGN RATIONALE: The clothing fuses the sunny, childlike qualities of folk art with high fashion. The fixtures are designed to resemble steamer trunks and are light in colour in order to cleanly display an assortment of colours, patterns and pieces. The store features a neutral envelope with intersecting soffiting and graphic highlights so that the merchandise stands out. The fixtures are crafted from maple, with silk-screened patterns that relate to the clothing

FIXTURE AND SIGN FABRICATORS: Design Fabricators, Inc.

PHOTOGRAPHER: Balthazar Korab

micro
QUASI
TEEN
HAPPY TO GROW UP

Comoni S.P.A.

COUNTRY OF ORIGIN: Italy

DESIGNER: Alex Fornari/Art Force S.R.L., Parma, Italy

DATE: 1994

TYPE OF IDENTITY IMPLEMENTATION: Logo for a line of children's apparel

TARGET AUDIENCE: Children aged 6–11 years

CLIENT'S BRIEF: Micro Store, a subsidiary of Comoni S.P.A. wanted to introduce a 'Quasi-Teen' (almost teenager market) line of clothing. Therefore a new logo had to be created

DESIGN RATIONALE: Using bold graphics and primary colours, a striking and accessible logo was designed and applied to all aspects of the identity

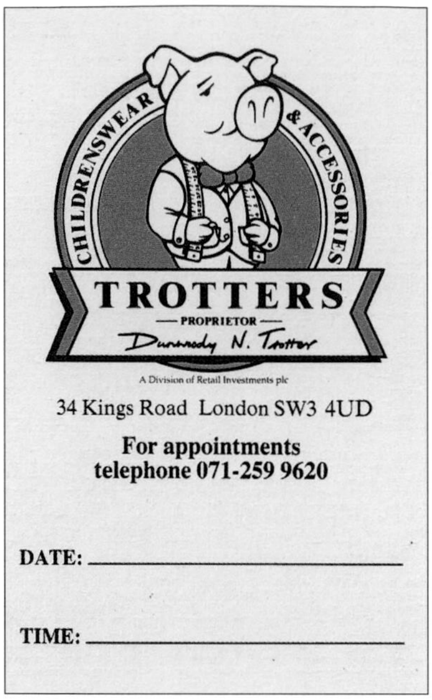

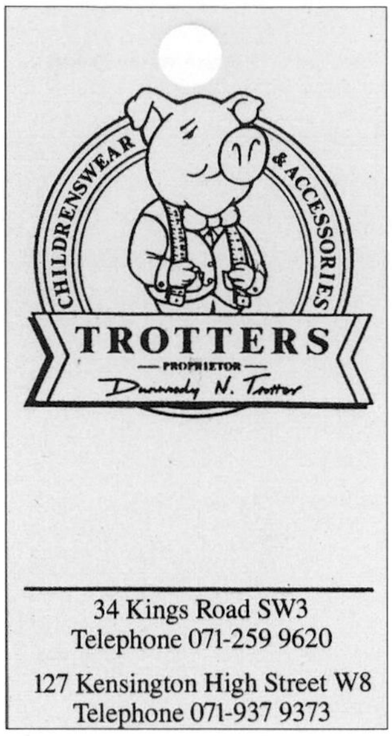

Trotters

COUNTRY OF ORIGIN: United Kingdom

DESIGNER: Richard Ross

DATE: 1990 October

TYPE OF IDENTITY IMPLEMENTATION: Complete identity

TARGET AUDIENCE: 0–8 year olds and their parents

CLIENT'S BRIEF: To create a shopping environment which was fun both for the children and adults

DESIGN RATIONALE: From previous design experience Richard Ross learned that the image of a 'pig' was the most successful animal at attracting both children and adults hence the pig motif. The name 'Trotters' was based on a sign found with the name 'Dunwoody N. Trotters'. The shops separates each area by themes, in one corner a hairdressing service is offered, in another books and another, toys. The colours selected emphasise the light-heartedness of the identity, whilst remaining unthreatening and warm

CHILDRENSWEAR
& ACCESSORIES
TROTTERS
PROPRIETOR
Dunwody N. Trotter
34 KINGS ROAD LONDON SW3 0171 259 9620
127 KENSINGTON HIGH STREET LONDON W8 0171 937 9373

SHOES

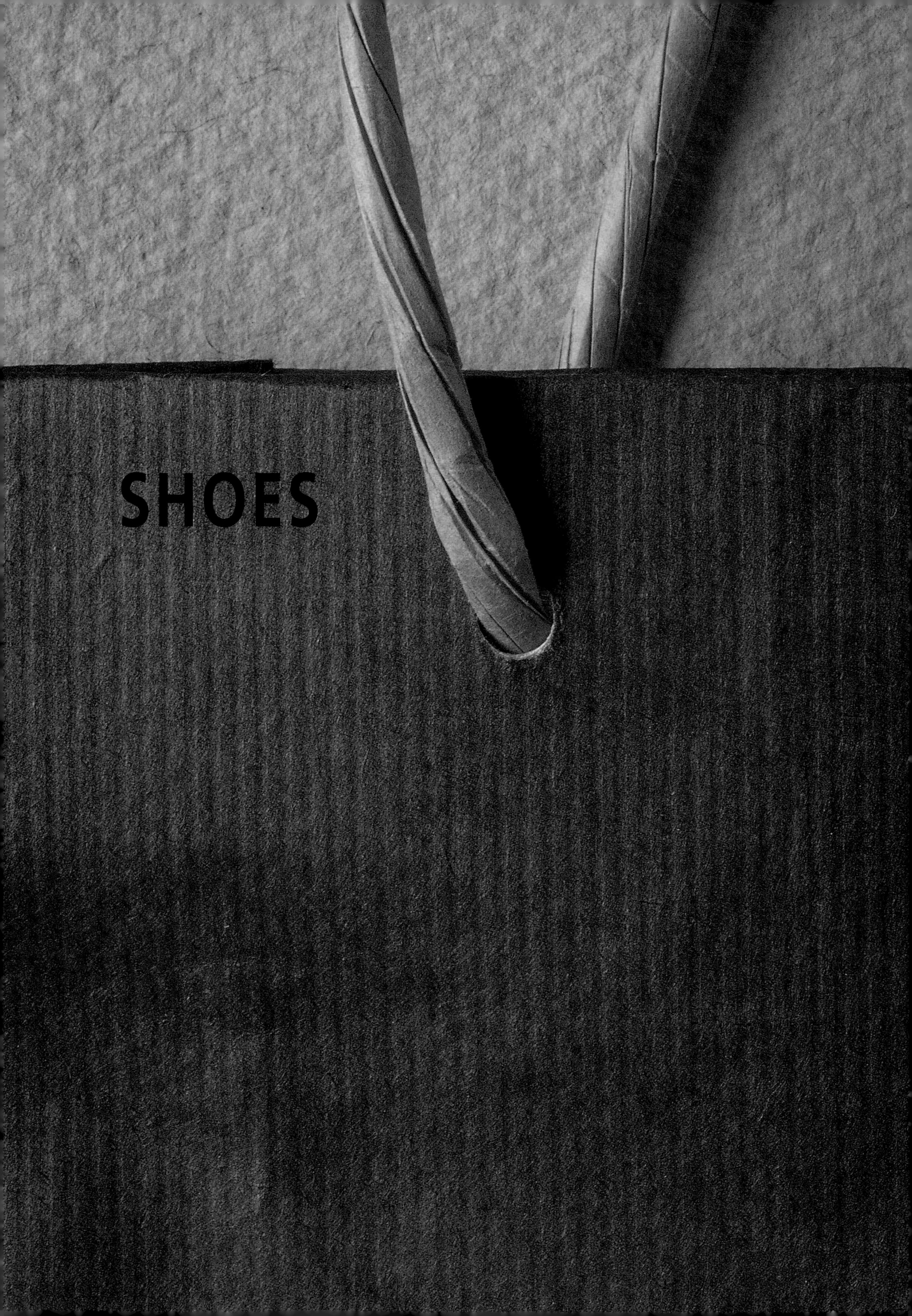

5

Stride Rite Inc.

COUNTRY OF ORIGIN: America

DESIGNER: John Lutz, Robin Perkins, Michele Phelan, Clifford Selbert/Clifford Selbert Design Collaborative, Cambridge, Massachusetts, USA

DATE: 1995 Spring

TYPE OF IDENTITY IMPLEMENTATION: Store design and logo generation

TARGET AUDIENCE: Mothers aged 25–45 years

CLIENT'S BRIEF: To develop a cohesive and consistent brand identity at retail and wholesale level

DESIGN RATIONALE: Simple forms, illustrations and a very basic colour palette that is bold and cheerful were used. The square was applied as a simple system that is carried throughout from 2-D to 3-D design

ILLUSTRATOR: Gerry Bustamante

PHOTOGRAPHER: Anton Grassl

toddlers

stride rite

Dolcis

COUNTRY OF ORIGIN: United Kingdom
DESIGNER: 20/20 Design and Strategy Consultants, London, England
DATE: 1995 April
TYPE OF IDENTITY IMPLEMENTATION: All elements
TARGET AUDIENCE: 12–24 years

CLIENT'S BRIEF: To place Dolcis as the young fashion footwear leader in the high street – ahead of the competition and fashion clothing competitors. To create a new store concept that positions Dolcis as a fashion business that sells shoes – not just a shoe shop that sells fashionable merchandise

DESIGN RATIONALE: Every time customers step into the new concept Dolcis we want them to feel as though they have walked onto the set of 'The Word' or 'into' their favourite magazine. The window displays are bold fashion stories not dozens of shoes lined like birds on a telephone wire. Once inside the store is divided into mens and women's areas – each

segmented to reflect their different shopping 'mindsets'. Punctuating each respective area, are bold 'hot spot' zones – highlighting the latest look or appropriate product story. A new service coda was created driven around the service bar around which monitors pump out MTV and catwalk shows *(continued on pp.166-7)*

dar
wear
orgasmic

dolcis
R
WAVES

m
w
orgasmic

sole
chart
cool
CANVAS
cool
SUMMER
dolcis
R
ea
WAVES
spring 1995

Shoe Express

COUNTRY OF ORIGIN: United Kingdom

DESIGNER: Gordon Orr, David Sparkes/Sparkes Orr Design Consultants, London, England

DATE: 1993 November

TYPE OF IDENTITY IMPLEMENTATION: Corporate identity, fascia, internal graphics, point-of-sale, carrier bags, shoe boxes

TARGET AUDIENCE: Lower end of the retail market

CLIENT'S BRIEF: To design a self-service shoe store with the shoes displayed in boxes. To offer quality and value in male, female and children's shoes

DESIGN RATIONALE: The store communicated its offer through the name (which Sparkes Orr created) and colour of its external image. No display was envisaged although by keeping the windows clear, shoppers are able to see inside and understand the offer at a glance

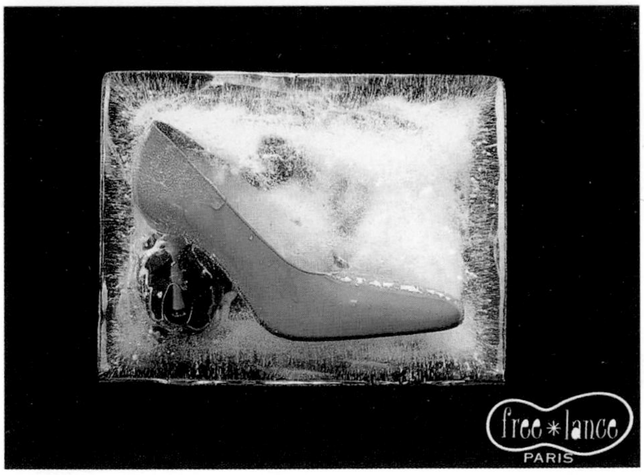

Freelance

COUNTRY OF ORIGIN: United Kingdom

DESIGNER: John Eager, London, England

DATE: 1995 April

TYPE OF IDENTITY IMPLEMENTATION: Complete identity

TARGET AUDIENCE: Well-heeled style gurus

CLIENT'S BRIEF: To create an identity to appeal to the affluent as well as the average shoe shopper. To maintain an up-beat image whilst reflecting the quality and unique designs of the shoes themselves

DESIGN RATIONALE: A sharp 90's street scope design mix of wrought-iron and striking damask sofas combines Bill Amberg's leather floor design to form an extraordinary shoe retailing platform

Cable & Co/ British Shoe Corporation

COUNTRY OF ORIGIN: United Kingdom

DESIGNER: Davies/Baron, London, England

DATE: 1995 January–February

TYPE OF IDENTITY IMPLEMENTATION: Fascia, internal signage, stationery, carrier bags, swing tickets, packaging, point-of-sale

TARGET AUDIENCE: General public

CLIENT'S BRIEF: To update the retail design concept created by Davis/Baron in 1987 and apply the blue print to the prototype store in the Metro Centre, Newcastle. To work to a very tight deadline

DESIGN RATIONALE: Elegant and classical typeface was chosen. Gold on deep burgundy created a warmth and expensive feel, lifting Cable & Co. out of the lower end of the shoe market and into the more affluent one

CABLE & Co
CABLE & Co
1901

CABLE & Co
E & Co
CABLE & Co
1901

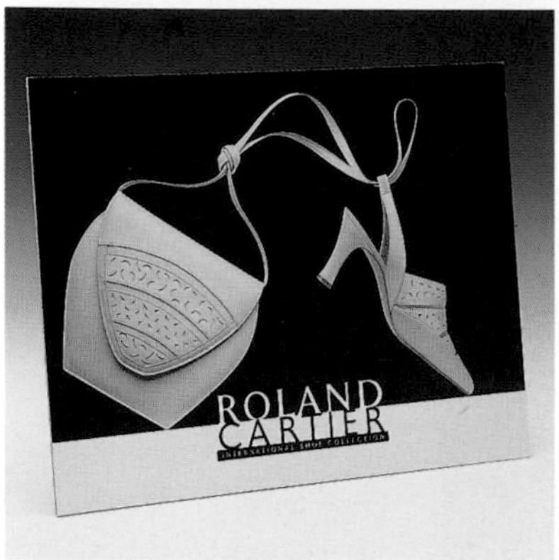

Roland Cartier

COUNTRY OF ORIGIN: United Kingdom

DESIGNER: Derek Martin, Gary Moore, Justin Southgate/Parker Stratton Design, London, England

DATE: 1995 August

TYPE OF IDENTITY IMPLEMENTATION: Logo, ticketing, labels, bags, stationery, folders, fascia, folders, internal signage, interior, point-of-sale, card scheme

TARGET AUDIENCE: 35 year old women

CLIENT'S BRIEF: 'People either loved the brand or hated it. We wanted more people to love it' (James Walker, British Shoe Brands Marketing Controller). To update an existing brand and broaden the appeal to new customers

DESIGN RATIONALE: A new brand identity was created that reflected core values of glamour, sophistication, quality and excitement to appeal to women whose every moment is a special occasion

ART DIRECTOR: Martina Langer

COPYWRITER: David Watkinson

INTERIOR:David Bentheim

PHOTOGRAPHERS: Richard Glover (Interiors) and Steve Wakeham (Gra phics)

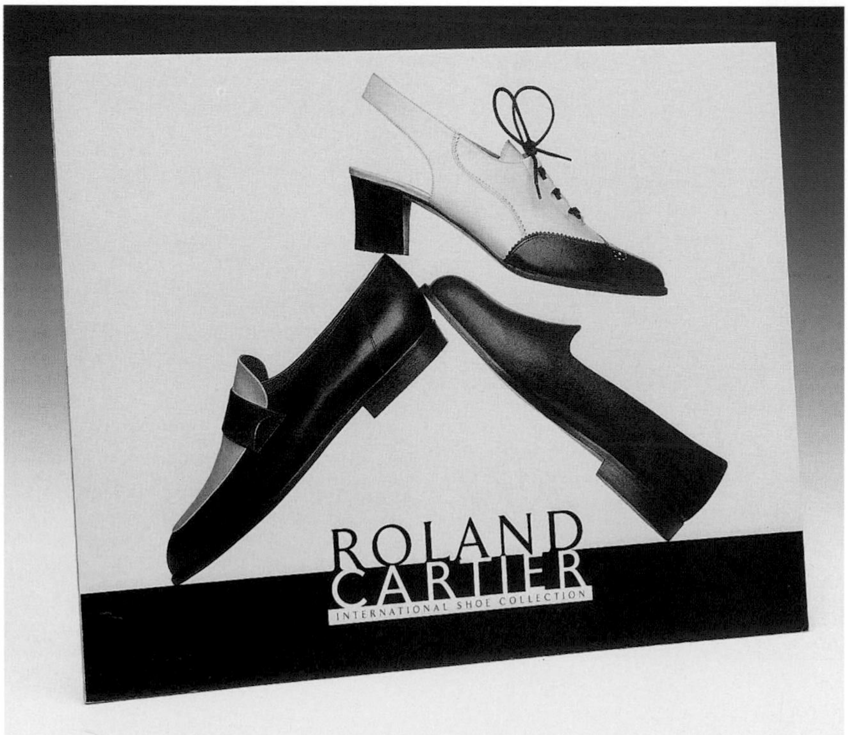

(continued on pp.174-5)

ROLAND
CARTIER
INTERNATIONAL SHOE COLLECTION

ROLAND
CARTIER
INTERNATIONAL SHOE COLLECTION
RC

OLAND
ARTIER
ATIONAL SHOE COLLECTION

Gina Shoes

COUNTRY OF ORIGIN: United Kingdom
DESIGNER: Kate Goode/The Trigger Foundation, London, England
DATE: 1993
TYPE OF IDENTITY IMPLEMENTATION: Logo, letterheads, bags
TARGET AUDIENCE: The higher spending market
CLIENT'S BRIEF: To create a new identity for an exclusive range of shoes
DESIGN RATIONALE: The existing identity was reworked, the shape of the shoe was manipulated to create a modern yet elegant and eye-catching logo in rich and elegant colours of purple and gold

GINA

Shellys

COUNTRY OF ORIGIN: United Kingdom

DESIGNER: Adrian Kilby/The Formation Creative Consultants, London, England

DATE: 1995 July

TYPE OF IDENTITY IMPLEMENTATION: Product signage, merchandising, logo, shop windows, internal signage

TARGET AUDIENCE: Fashion conscious 16–25 year olds

CLIENT'S BRIEF: To develop a merchandising identity that expresses the originality of Shellys shoes and allows other brands to be promoted in store with the Shellys endorsement. To produce creative point-of-sale for both Shellys and other brands sold in store

DESIGN RATIONALE: The identity is based around a thumbprint 'sole' incorporating the famous Shellys oval with a changeable heel print. The logo embodies both the originality of the designs and the individualism of the wearer. The changeable heelprint allows other brands to carry their own

identity yet retain the Shellys endorsement. The point-of-sale graphics draw their inspiration from famous works of art. The paintings link two unique creations in an irreverent and humorous way. Like the original paintings, each Shellys shoe design is a work of art in its own right

ILLUSTRATOR: Martin Joyce
INTERIOR DESIGNER: Steve Turner
METAL SHOE DISPLAYS: Jamie Hart
SHOP FITTINGS: Tienda Services Ltd, England

Bally

COUNTRY OF ORIGIN: Switzerland

DESIGNER: Martin Gaberthüel, Antonie Reinhard, Andrea Reinhart/Seiler DDB Needham, Berne, Switzerland

DATE: 1993 January

TYPE OF IDENTITY IMPLEMENTATION: All elements (except logo)

TARGET AUDIENCE: Fashion conscious, discriminating people worldwide, higher income

CLIENT'S BRIEF: To revitalise the brand, to express high quality, fashionable classic designs, at a higher price

DESIGN RATIONALE: The result is an elegant, rather understated design, using the revised existing and well known logo. A distinguished colour scheme which outlasts seasonal fashion trends and represents the high standard of the brand and its customers is used

SHOP DESIGN: Andree Putman/Ecart

Leisure

Classic

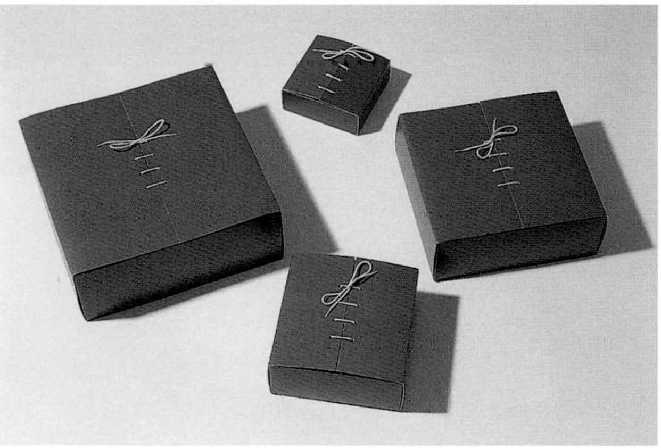

Gift

Size (Reading)

COUNTRY OF ORIGIN: United Kingdom

DESIGNER: Kulbir Chadha/Kulbir Chadha Architecture, London, England

DATE: 1993 November

TYPE OF IDENTITY IMPLEMENTATION: Shop fittings, internal and external signage, bags, shoe tags, shoe boxes, business cards

TARGET AUDIENCE: Fashionable youth 15–35 year-olds

CLIENT'S BRIEF: To target the audience with an invigorating, fresh, vibrant image with many sources including ethnic, modern and future culture, the industrial and pop/club culture

DESIGN RATIONALE: The four lettered name 'size' is intended to catch on as a 'buzz' word. A language of scale is introduced in the design – similar objects but of different sizes. 'Size' is used as a metaphor for the individual. An eclectic approach was adopted in the use of geometry, colour and space but one that is constantly altered with the personalities of the objects and users

DESIGN TEAM: Alan Farlie, Pedro Haberbosch, Duncan Woodburn

PHOTOGRAPHER: Tom Miller

Happy Valentine's

Size (Hammersmith)

COUNTRY OF ORIGIN: United Kingdom
DESIGNER: Kulbir Chadha/Kulbir Chadha Architecture, London, England
DATE: 1994 February
TYPE OF IDENTITY IMPLEMENTATION: Shop fittings, signage, carrier bags
TARGET AUDIENCE: Fashionable youth 15–35 years
CLIENT'S BRIEF: To continue the theme from Size Reading, to encourage browsing with greater window display, to utilise the low budget to advantage by the honest expression of raw materials
DESIGN RATIONALE: The 80's granite clad building that the shop is set in is mocked for the superficiality of its high quality finishes. The true construction of the building spills out in the form of the air-conditioning duct steel sheeting, the concrete floor and ceiling and the raw scaffolding timber. The corner location of the shop is enhanced by the circular geometry. The colour scheme is left neutral to allow the future projection of slides, film and coloured lights on the bare white walls
ADDITIONAL CREDITS: Pedro Haberbosch

(continued on pp. 184/5)

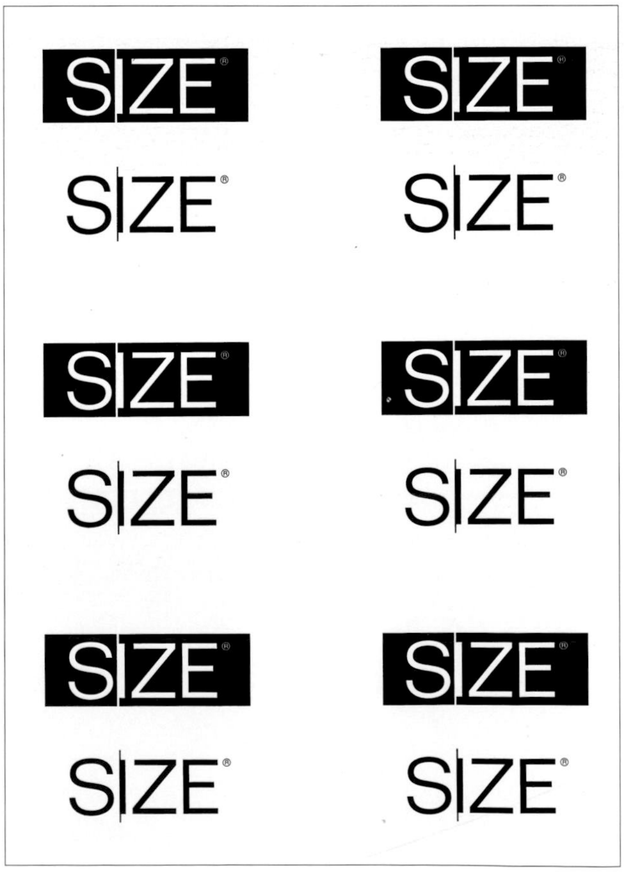

SIZE

Camper

COUNTRY OF ORIGIN: Spain
DESIGNER: Neville Brody and Simon Griffin/Research Studios, London, England
DATE: 1995 October
TYPE OF IDENTITY IMPLEMENTATION: Stationery, bags, shoe tags, T-shirts, exterior and interior signage, shoe boxes, advertising
TARGET AUDIENCE: 15–40 year olds
CLIENT'S BRIEF: The company has been in existence for twenty-five years and needed to have a more contemporary design to suit global expansion
DESIGN RATIONALE: A thoroughly modern and global identity was created to match the age group and the various languages of each outlet. This makes the design unique since it talks to an international audience and fits into any environment. The design is expected to remain unaltered for ten years
PHOTOGRAPHER: Rod Howe

Camper U.K Launch Party
R.S.V.P
Please Tick as appropriate.
Yes, I will be attending the Camper U.K Launch Party.
No, I will be unable to attend the Camper U.K Launch Party.
camper c
Ruth Coughlan
Press & Public Relations
1-4 Langley Court,
Covent Garden,
London, WC2E 9JY.
Tel: 0171 379 7500
Fax: 0171 379 7515

Camper U.K Launch Party
Camper the Spanish Tradition in Men's and Ladies footwear would like to invite you to the debut unveiling of our new London Shop.
The Time: 6-8pm. Thursday 19th October 1995,
The Place: Our new shop. 39 Floral Street, Covent Garden, WC2.
Our European Flagship in the heart of London's Covent Garden.

camper
Coflusa S.A. Poligono Industrial s/n . 07300 Inca . Mallorca . Spain . Tel 971-50 35 00 . Fax 971-50 47 02

camper
Antonio Socías
Polígono Industrial s/n
07300 Inca .
Mallorca . Spain
Tel 971-503500
Fax 971-504702

BANKS & BUILDING SOCIETIES

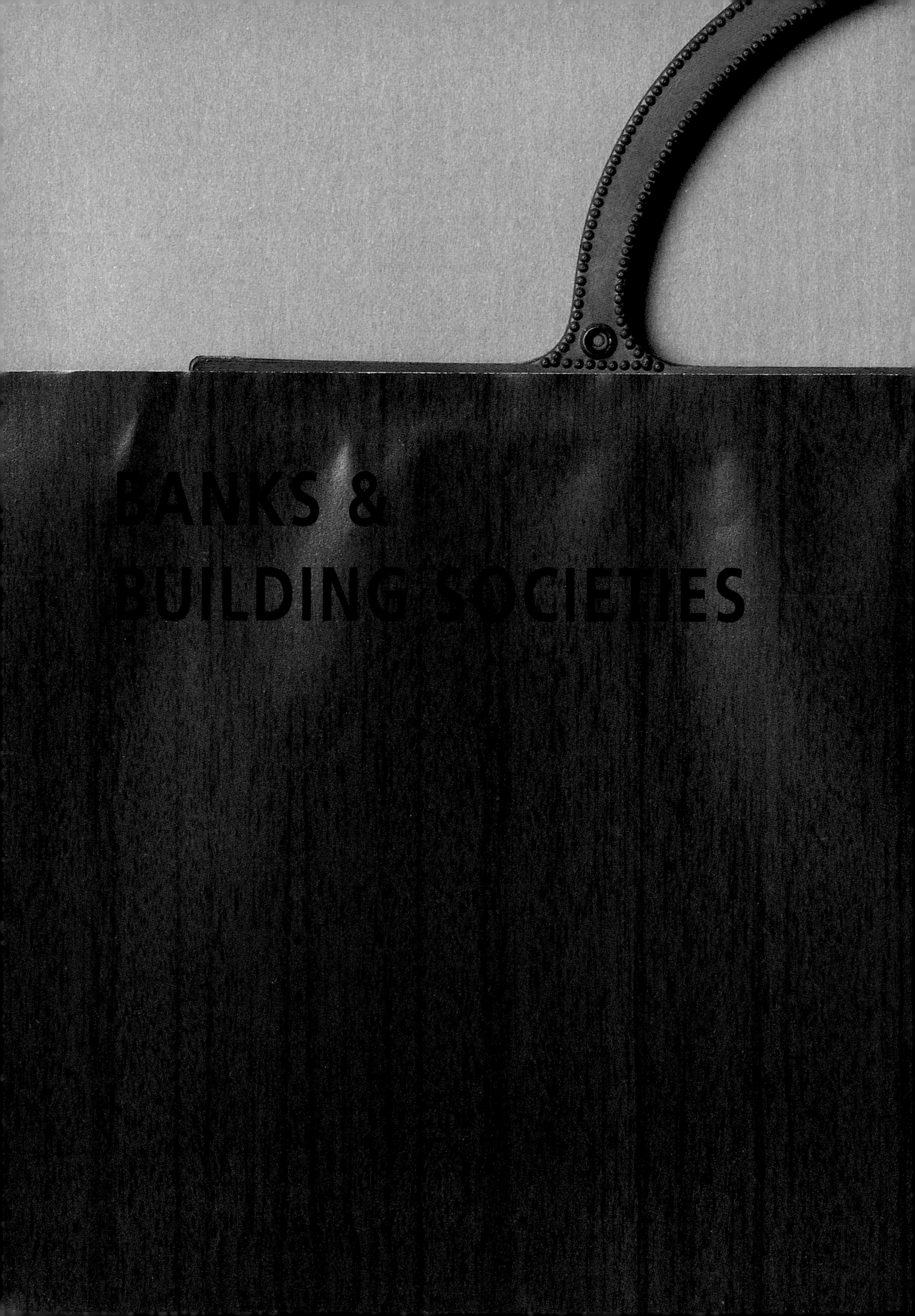

6

ING Bank

COUNTRY OF ORIGIN: The Netherlands

DESIGNER: Nick Butcher, Christian Davies/Fitch, London, England

DATE: 1993 April–May

TYPE OF IDENTITY IMPLEMENTATION: Elements relating to the automated service

CLIENT'S BRIEF: To create fully-automated local branches without losing the warmth and interface elements of normal, staffed branches. To offer the maximum services and information in a brightly-lit, welcoming environment so combining the offers of the traditional automated lobby and the staffed branch

DESIGN RATIONALE: Each automated branch has four main areas. Firstly, the shopfront, revealing the interior which has a night safe facility for business deposits. Inside, the transaction area, offers cashpoint and cheque-printing facilities as well as an interactive 'Link' screen. The 'Link' provides information on all aspects of personal banking, shows the location of main branches by map and enables the customer to request a meeting with the bank staff or order a statement. The most radical offer is the ability to let the customer talk to the manager at a larger branch by intercom. Thirdly, there is a central reading and writing area, a soft and calm environment for banking business. A final area uses posters to display a range banking services geared to the customer

PHOTOGRAPHER: John Linden

Uw Geld
Opnemen en Saldo-opvragen
Uw Cheques
Afhalen
Informatie voor u

Uw Geld
nemen en Saldo-opvragen
Uw Cheques
Afhalen

Solo

COUNTRY OF ORIGIN: Finland

DESIGNER: Tay Chong Huang/Wolff Olins, London, England

DATE: 1991 May

TYPE OF IDENTITY IMPLEMENTATION: Brand identity and positioning, signage, brochures, credit cards, posters, retail scheme

CLIENT'S BRIEF: To take the lead in electronic banking and to improve the bank's image

DESIGN RATIONALE: The bold use of colours and lettering removed any confusing elements and hoped to strike the customer immediately. The electronic features provided by this bank for its customers are contained in simple yet stylish information display systems

Solo-asiakkaana hoidat päivittäiset raha-asiasi silloin, kun sinulle sopii.
Uusi kortti Sinulle, joka olet 7 vaan et 15 vuotta.
Kortti, jolla saa rahaa automaateista.
Kortti, joka opettaa raha-asioiden viisasta hoitoa.
Kortti, joka kertoo SYP:n asiakkuudesta.
Kortti, jota kehtaa näyttää ja käyttää.
Kortti, johon liittyy etuja.
Se on Smartcard.

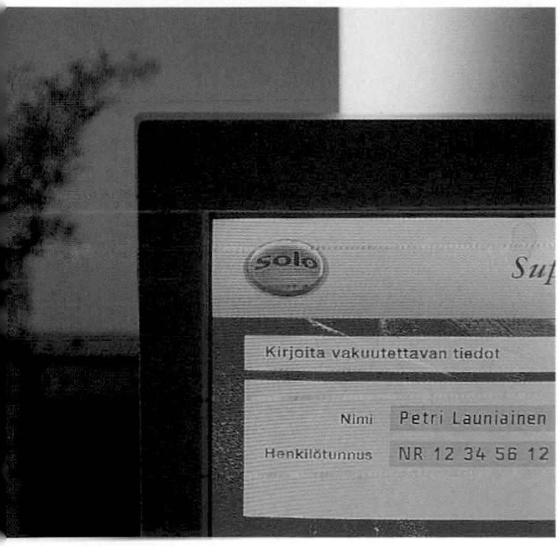
Kirjoita vakuutettavan tiedot
Nimi
Petri Launiainen
Henkilötunnus
NR 12 34 56 12

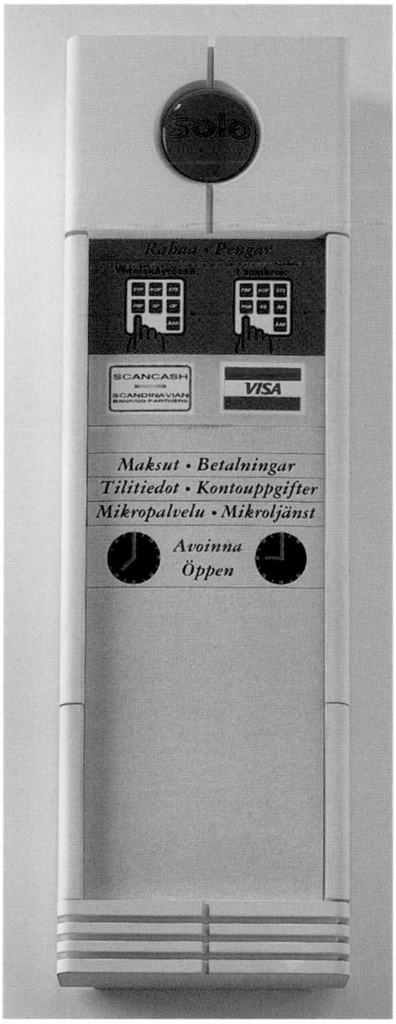
Rahaa • Pengar
SCANCASH
SCANDINAVIAN
VISA
Maksut • Betalningar
Tilitiedot • Kontouppgifter
Mikropalvelu • Mikroljänst
Avoinna
Öppen

Finanssitietopalvelut
YHDYSPANKKI

Royal Bank of Scotland

COUNTRY OF ORIGIN: United Kingdom

DESIGNER: Davies/Baron, London, England

DATE: 1995 April

TYPE OF IDENTITY IMPLEMENTATION: Fascia, point-of-sale, literature, stationery, interior and exterior

TARGET AUDIENCE: Existing and new customers

CLIENT'S BRIEF: To develop a retail brand positioning and visual style to differentiate Royal Bank and add value tofinancial products and services

DESIGN RATIONALE: An entirely new visual language has been created. In effect, a three-dimensional corporate identity encompassing retail branding. The overall design package has been created to be totally flexible and modular, allowing for easy and inexpensive refreshment of the environment

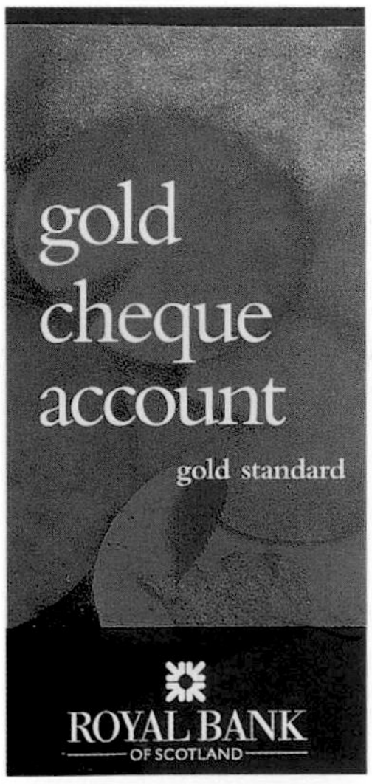

The Royal Bank of Scotland
mortgage shop
The Royal Bank of Scotland
mortgage shop
mortgage shop
The Royal Bank mortgage that won't go up, but can come down.
Capped Rate mortgages
The Royal Bank of Scotland plc
218 Union Street

ROYAL BANK
OF SCOTLAND

Cash up to £500

Bristol & West Building Society

COUNTRY OF ORIGIN: United Kingdom
DESIGNER: John Davies/John Davies Design, Buckinghamshire, England
DATE: 1995 September
TYPE OF IDENTITY IMPLEMENTATION: Offices, external and internal signage, stationery, brochures, leaflets, point-of-sale units, Microsoft systems (slide presentations), direct marketing and advertising
TARGET AUDIENCE: All potential savers or borrowers, existing and younger customers
CLIENT'S BRIEF: To create a single Bristol & West brand, integrating the Tilney Lumsden Shane interior concept with the 'faces' logo by Indigo Design. To apply it economically and uniformly across all manifestations of the Society's image and to create a sub-branding structure for all Bristol & West products and services
DESIGN RATIONALE: Existing concepts related to large purpose built branches across different retail brands. The 'Bristol & West' brand was achieved by uniform presentation across many different styles of the branches, the consistency of application of the 'logo' and related typefaces on all the society's imagery
ADDITIONAL CREDITS: Ian Lettuce (Design Manual)
INTERIORS: Tilney Lumsden Shane, England
INTERIOR AND EXTERIOR SIGNAGE: Bovis Southwest Ltd

BRISTOL & WEST
BRISTOL & WEST BUILDING SOCIETY
MORTGAGE SAVINGS INVESTMENTS

Argentaria

COUNTRY OF ORIGIN: Spain

DESIGNER: Twelve Stars Communications Ltd, London, England

DATE: 1995

TYPE OF IDENTITY IMPLEMENTATION: Logo, letterheads, business cards, promotional material

CLIENT'S BRIEF: The Corporación Bancaria de Espana (CBE) was created when all of Spain's state-owned financial institutions were united to form a single banking corporation. In preparation for CBE's privatisation and market expansion, a structure that would group all units under one vision and to signal a unique market-driven positioning was desired

DESIGN RATIONALE: This federal banking structure allowed each of the individual business units to maintain their own specialisation and client base while unifying under a common umbrella (2,000 different brands were united under the Argentaria brand). Twelve Stars coined the name Argentaria from the Latin name for a bank used 2,000 years ago across the Roman Empire. The new name gives Argentaria the flexibility of attracting a wider international audience. A unique translucent yellow tone was used to differentiate Argentaria from its competitors at a retail level. Twelve Stars teamed up with 3M to develop the material for the translucent signage

ARGENTARIA

BANCO
irecto
ARGENTARIA
HABLE
CON
EL BANCO.
Una nueva tecnología bancaria y un eficaz servicio
han hecho posible. El primer banco directo del país.
El Banco abierto las 24 horas del día, 365 días al año.
ara realizar todo tipo de operaciones bancarias,
ando usted lo decida, desde su casa.
Sólo con una llamada telefónica.
Ser cliente del Banco Directo es beneficiarse de todos
los servicios del primer grupo bancario y financiero
del país.
ARGENTARIA es el Banco Exterior, Caja Postal,
Banco Hipotecario, Banco de Crédito Local,
Banco de Crédito Agrícola, Banco de Negocios Argentaria,
Banco Directo, Banco Simeón, Banco Alicante, BGF,
Hércules Seguros, SVB Argentaria y otras Sociedades
Financieras y de Seguros.
ARGENTARIA la nueva generación de banca.
ARGENTARIA
Corporación Bancaria de España

SHOPPING
CENTRES

7

Centre Court Shopping Centre

COUNTRY OF ORIGIN: England

DESIGNER: Richard Dragun, Martin Roy/BDP Design, London, England

DATE: 1993

TYPE OF IDENTITY IMPLEMENTATION: Signage

TARGET AUDIENCE: General public

CLIENT'S BRIEF: To design a logo and signage scheme that projected the new use of existing buildings which had been incorporated into a brand new scheme whilst respecting the historic associations of the site

DESIGN RATIONALE: The comprehensive graphic programme drew inspiration from a glazed rotunda entrance for its logo. The decorative nature of the internal signs complement the rich and diverse finishes and materials used within the scheme

SIGNMAKER: John Anthony Signs, England

Café
COURT

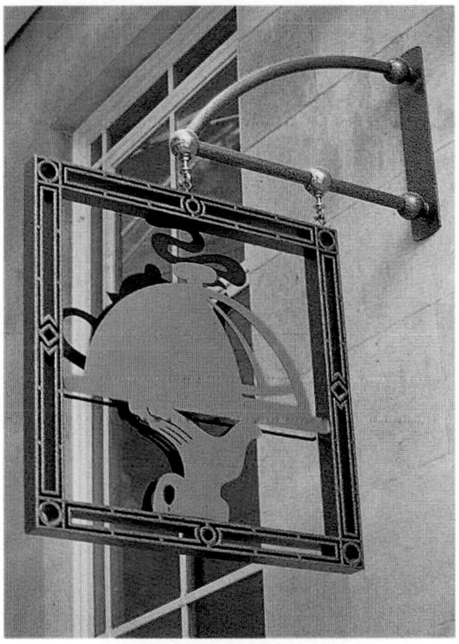

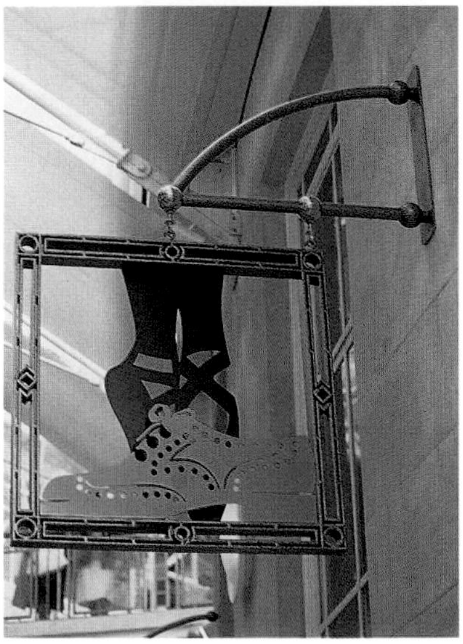

Brandon Town Centre

COUNTRY OF ORIGIN: America

DESIGNER: Robert Wingard/RTKL Associates Inc., Baltimore, Maryland, USA

DATE: 1995 February

TYPE OF IDENTITY IMPLEMENTATION: Exterior and interior signage, sculpture

TARGET AUDIENCE: General public

CLIENT'S BRIEF: To create a one-level retail centre, to provide a lively retail core for centre of Brandon

DESIGN RATIONALE: The centre reflects the local architecture with its decorated red brick façades and five steeple-like towers which announce the interior vaulted malls and courts. The combination of roof skylights and clerestories flood the interiors

with natural light while providing shade from intense sunlight. The central court is vast yet inviting with a vaulted roof, two and a half stories high with exposed steel trusses trimmed in bright colours. A large central fountain and twelve smaller ones provide a soothing respite from the bustle of shopping. Architectural and environmental graphic design characterise the directional and decorative elements inspired by alligators, geckos, mantees and other wildlife indigenous to Florida

PHOTOGRAPHER: David Whitcomb
PROJECT MANAGER: Charles Greenland/
RTKL Associates, Inc.
SCULPTOR: Jo Schneider

Gyle Shopping Centre Development

COUNTRY OF ORIGIN: Scotland

DESIGNER: Andrew Hunter, Rory McNeill, Martin Tilley/McIlroy Coates Ltd, Edinburgh, Scotland

DATE: 1993 October

TYPE OF IDENTITY IMPLEMENTATION: External and internal signage, stationery, marketing literature

TARGET AUDIENCE: General public

CLIENT'S BRIEF: To design a complex to convey the quality and plurality of the developers within the centre and the rich choice of goods they sell

DESIGN RATIONALE: From the 'E' of Gyle sprang an elegant logo type, the environmental signage system was essential for its effective functioning. This system uses monolithic slab type signs, designed to compliment the architectural integrity of the centre, it is aesthetically innovative yet highly functional. The Gyle was awarded European Centre of the Year, the first in Britain

INFORMATION

F2

51 LOCKER

FOOD COURT

The Plaza at West Covina

COUNTRY OF ORIGIN: America

DESIGNER: Paul F. Jacob III, Howard M. Kurushima/ RTKL Associates Inc., Baltimore, Maryland, USA

DATE: 1993 October

TYPE OF IDENTITY IMPLEMENTATION: Exterior and interior signage, mall collateral material

TARGET AUDIENCE: General public

CLIENT'S BRIEF: To expand and renovate the existing plaza using environmental graphics and local icons, to create an exciting atmosphere in which to shop

DESIGN RATIONALE: Local icons – a spiral, walnut leaf, oak leaf and sun – with colourful cut-aluminium interpretations of these elements were used throughout the mall. This playful scheme included whimsical versions of 'dogs', 'cows' and 'mice' and these also appear as decorative lighting features. The façade is translucent. The interior lamp posts are topped with illuminated acorns and little 'creatures' sit on top of lighting fixtures and signs, wall sconces are shaped into swirls and leaves. Graphic features are adjustable and enable lighting (either fluorescent or incandescent) to be aimed directly onto the graphic elements, solidifying the relationship between lighting and design

GRAPHICS: Frank Christian, Ann Dudrow, Phillips S. Engelke, Charles Greenawalt/RTKL Associates Inc.

PHOTOGRAPHER: Scott McDonald/Heinrich-Blessing, USA and David Whitcomb

TLE ACORN,
TREE-TO
GREAT O

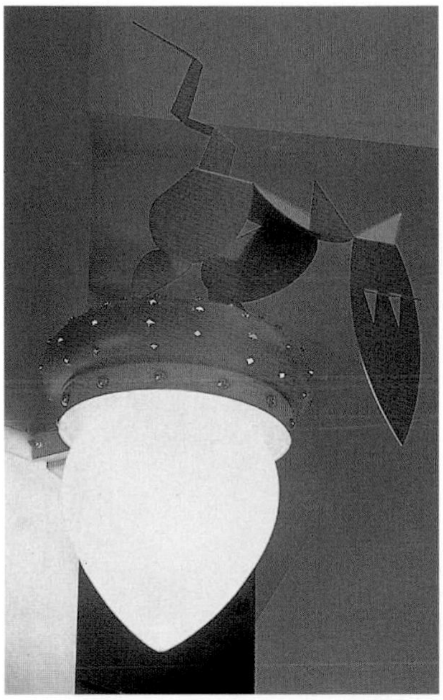

HOVERING
GLIDING

ATT

COUNTRY OF ORIGIN: Taiwan

DESIGNER: Valerie Wickes/DIN Graphics, London, England

DATE: 1993 January

TYPE OF IDENTITY IMPLEMENTATION: Bags, signage, fascia, stationery, clothing

TARGET AUDIENCE: 16–40 year olds

CLIENT'S BRIEF: To create an identity that had a strong European influence, a slightly 'clubby' feel and 'magazine' quality. The new identity had to be dynamic and youthful and appeal equally to men and women

DESIGN RATIONALE: A strong, clear graphic symbol was adopted; a dynamic shape that echoed the spirit of a European club or magazine. The shop is open almost twenty-four hours a day and a 'buzz' is created by the use of its graphics and fascia

(continued on pp. 218-21)

PEBBLES

AS

STU. 312
STU
312
STU
312
STU
312
STU
312
STU
3-2

3-2

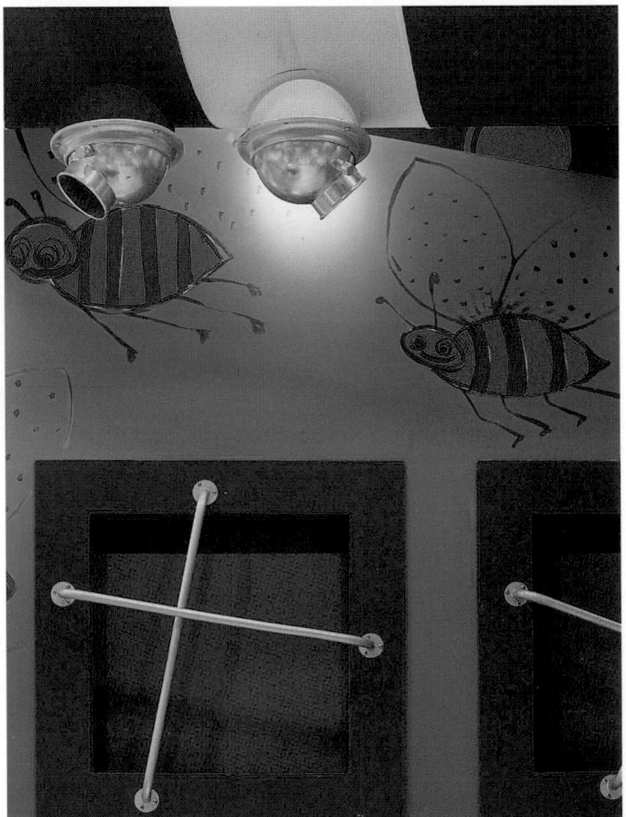

THE V CLUB

Index of Projects